QUEENS IN SAND CASTLES

2ND EDITION

Published by MRW Publishing 2024
Copyright © Tracy Tully

ISBN
Paperback - 978-0-6453330-4-6
Ebook - 978-0-6453330-5-3

 A catalogue record for this book is available from the National Library of Australia

All Rights Reserved. No part of this book may be reproduced by any mechanical, photographic, or electronic processes, or in the form of a phonographic recording. Nor may it be stored in a retrieval system, transmitted, or otherwise copied for public or private use other than for 'fair use' (as brief quotations embodied in articles and reviews) without prior written permission of the publisher.

Disclaimer - The information in this book is designed to provide helpful information on the subjects discussed. This information is not meant to be used, nor should it be used, to diagnose or treat any medical condition. For diagnosis or treatment for any medical condition, consult your own physician. The publisher and authors are not responsible for any specific health or mental health needs that may require medical supervision and are not liable for any damages or negative consequences from any treatment, action, application, or preparation to any person reading or following the information in this book.

References are provided for informational purposes only and do not constitute endorsement of any website, books, or other sources. Readers should be aware that the information in the book shared by the individual authors is their unique story, and the publisher is not liable for any damages, consequences or mental health needs that may require medical supervision and are not liable for any damages or negative consequences from any treatment, action, application, or preparation to any person reading or following the information in this book.

Without in any way limiting the authors' and publisher's exclusive rights under copyright any use of this publication to "train" generative artificial intelligence (AI) technologies to generate text is expressly prohibited. The authors' reserve all rights to license uses of this work for generative AI training and development of machine learning language models.

Illustrated by: Margo Bobrowicz

QUEENS IN SAND CASTLES

2ND EDITION

A CO-AUTHOR COLLABORATION

Caroline Bellinger, Andrea Putting, Lara Zelenka,
Tiffany Droge, Sam Dean, Sam Beckman, Jean-Marcel
Eliézer Malliaté, Joy Allardyce and Tracy Tully

MRW PUBLISHING

CONTENTS

LIVING LIFE COURAGEOUSLY by CAROLINE BELLINGER	1
COLLABORATIVE PROSPERITY by ANDREA PUTTING	21
GIRL FINDS HER PURPOSE AND SOUL GRIT by LARA ZELENKA	43
MY MAGIC MIKE MOMENT by TIFFANY DROGE	63
BECOMING THE ALIGNED LEADER THE ANSWER: LEADERSHIP FATIGUE SYNDROME by SAM DEAN	85
TWO BENT RODS by SAM BECKMAN	107
FREEDOM & CHOICE by CO-AUTHOR MR. JEAN-MARCEL ELIÉZER MALLIATÉ MDR	129
COME FLY WITH ME ... ON A DC-3 by JOY ALLARDYCE	143
LOST AT SEA! CALIBRATE YOUR MINDSET ... FIND TRUE NORTH by TRACY TULLY	149
SHE RISES FROM THE FIRE A HEROIC PROSE by TRACY TULLY	165
BECOME A CO-AUTHOR!	167

To those fearless entrepreneurs, whose empowered attitude inspires others by sharing their individual passages from despair to success.

We wish our readers courage, fortitude, and resilience!

To those who have stood by us through the turbulent years, we thank you for supporting our endeavours and the words we penned in this book,
Queens in Sand Castles.

Together, we have brought to you our stories, thoughts, advice, and suggestions in the hope of sharing inspiration to each of our readers.

INTRODUCTION

QUEENS IN SAND CASTLES 2 is the second edition, inspired by the role that women have engaged in within their business organisations, the world over.

This outstanding title symbolises a woman's life in business, twisting and turning like the ebb and flow of water, smooth at one moment and treacherous the next.

Each chapter shares a business Queen's story of how they circumnavigated rocky storms in life, steering through the turbulence that caused chaos and turmoil. Through the author's words as they share the strategies, they used to achieve the calm in their business and lives.

Queens in Sand Castles was created as a collaboration. A Co-Author book to encourage and motivate those women in the lonely life of business as they navigate their journeys as a captain of their ships.

This book is designed to stimulate those in positions of value adding to others; the CEO, coach, consultant, entrepreneur, or agent.

YOUR QUEEN'S PRIORITY PLEDGE:

" I'm committed to improving myself by leveraging fear to build resilience.

Each time you feel fear, you become more skilled at understanding a deeper level of yourself. You have insight into your immediate reactions to unknown situations.

When your mind is confident, fear will diminish. It is then, that you will discover the power of self-awareness."
—Tracy Tully

Brought to you by MRW Publishing

1
LIVING LIFE COURAGEOUSLY

by CAROLINE BELLINGER

MY small stature bleached uneven hair, and hyena-like laugh characterise my fun, generous nature. Interestingly these features are often mistaken for someone who is a pushover and can be taken advantage of.

However, it only takes one look from my steely green eyes to know I mean business. When required, I like to be the underdog who dares to speak out courageously against injustice with the resilience to persevere through even the most challenging circumstances. I am curious about the world and have a bucket list full of adventures that I want to complete. I think the youth of today might say I have FOMO!

During one of those adventures, I pushed myself through limits that I never knew I could achieve. Even today, I sit here and think, "did I seriously do that?" But I have already said too much; let me go back to how it all began.

I have never been a talented or fast swimmer, but I remember those childhood days swimming up and down the black line in the local country swimming pool. It was over 40°C most summer days in the country town of Wycheproof, where I grew up, so the local pool was a hive of activity. My Mum was the swimming coach, so I do not think I really got much say about whether I did swim squad or not; I just had to do it. But I also remember how much fun we all had at the local pool lying around on the boiling hot concrete with friends as we sucked on ice-cold Glugs.

Over the years, I have continued swimming, but it has never been something I loved or was good at. In fact, I find the entire process of getting out of the pool, showered, dried, and changed quite tedious and annoying. When I started Triathlon a few years ago, I did a bit more swimming training. Still, running was my favourite discipline, cycling something I became pretty good at and swimming something I was forced to do at the start of a race. I think you might see a pattern emerging here. I do not really like swimming, and I'm not particularly that good at it. In fact, I consider myself to be the sloth of swimming.

I was born in a city and grew up most of my life in the country, so oceans were never a part of my experience except for the mandatory school holiday to the Gold Coast. I did spend quite a few years throughout my 20s and 30s living on the beach in Byron Bay and the Gold Coast. Still, to be honest, I saw way more of the inside of pubs and clubs than I ever did of the golden sandy beaches. The odd hangover ocean dip, but that is about it.

Fast forward to 2011, and I qualified in my Bronze Medallion to become a Surf Life Saver. I had recently got sober after a six-month stint in residential rehab, and I was looking for activities to keep me occupied and distracted. This may come as a bit of a shock to most of you, but you can be a surf lifesaver and have very basic swimming. Thank goodness for IRBs and rescue boards.

When the surf club started a social winter swim group, the "Cooly Cobias", I thought this would be an excellent opportunity to improve my ocean swimming. The social side of the swim and the hot soup afterwards was more motivating than a freezing cold swim in the ocean. Still, being one who always wanted a new adventure, I thought, why not give it a go. Since getting sober a few years earlier, I should also mention that I still suffered significant anxiety and depression and was slowly building up resilience and coping strategies. One of the things I feared the most, having not grown up in this environment, was ocean waves. At the start of every ocean swim, I would be overcome with anxiety. By the time my feet were in the water, my legs would be shaking from fear, and my heart rate would be pounding at a thousand knots. I would eventually dive in the water and under the incoming shore break waves. Still, I would be exhausted after about 100 m due to the anxiety and hormone overload that I had put myself through.

I would swim the weekly 1 km route panicking about each wave and then sit out the back beyond the break for about 10 minutes, trying to get the courage to swim back in through the wave break. I repeated this process every Sunday in winter for almost two years until one day. I was standing in the shallow water, getting ready to tackle those waves, when I realised that I was not feeling anxious. In fact, I was not that worried about the waves at all. It was one of those moments in life when you have an extraordinary realisation. For me, that realisation was that when I have anxiety, if I just keep pushing through and repeat repeatedly, eventually, my fear will either lessen or disappear altogether.

I have now been ocean swimming on a regular basis for about five years. And although I still swim like a sloth, I love being out in the ocean. I love the feel of salt water on my face and the movement of the sand as you swim over it. There is something incredibly tranquil and refreshing about being at one with the ocean. I don't even mind the occasional wave and strong sweep. It generally makes you swim faster and feel like an Olympian. So, when a few of my fellow swimmers mentioned a fun adventure swim around an Island, I was immediately curious. I should clarify that they are "swimmers" who swim the ocean several times a week and the pool every other day. And fast; they swim fast.

I read the brochure, and it mentioned crystal clear water and lots of turtles. The reality the swim was 3 km out to sea, a distance I have never swum, didn't even phase me. After all, the brochure said turtle watching and I was sold. We organised the surf club bus and a dozen of us heading up to the sunshine coast to swim around "Old Woman Island." Even the gender and age were on my side for this one.

Over the years, taking on many challenges in work, sport, and life, I have created quite a few strategies to alleviate any mental health concerns. During difficult times I implement my plans and get on with what I need to do. The negative impact of mental illness has lessened over the years, thanks to my personal development in this area. But my weakest moments are when I'm hormonal and stressed with a busy work agenda. The weekend of this swim just happened to coincide with my period and a successive few weeks of hectic work deadlines.

Being a bit OCD, I had checked the weather conditions all week, several times a day, on my phone app and discovered that the day of our swim was looking for a little bit unsettled. Constant looking at the forecast was not making the weather improve. Still, it certainly was having an impact on my anxiety levels.

So, when the bus finally arrived at our hotel, my state of anxiety was higher than I would have liked. For those who suffer, you will understand when I say that inner trembling was constant, and I was becoming more and more sensitive to noise and the environment. One of my strategies is to isolate and remove myself from excessive noise or activity whenever I feel like this. I also need to plan and prepare.

So, while everyone else was unpacking their bags, I snuck down the path beside the hotel and walked across the dunes to check out the ocean conditions. Immediate regret. As I looked south to Old Woman Island, 1 km out to sea, all I could see were massive white waves breaking on all sides of it. The conditions right in front of me were a significant shore break and rough. When I heard one of the elite swimmers mentioning how rough it was, I knew I was screwed.

After a restless night of no sleep, the following morning, we all trundled into the bus at 5 am and drove down to the event start location. I was feeling sick and wishing I had not decided to swim 3 km around a stupid island. I stopped talking and constantly reviewed in my mind what I was going to do. I did not HAVE to swim if the beach was too rough. If I struggled, there were going to be a lot of rescue boats and boards; I would just raise my hand and come straight back in.

As we lined up to register, I realised I had left my phone on charge at the hotel, which contained my registration and identification details. The universe was giving me an out option, and as I sighed with relief. That was short-lived as the lovely lady at the desk felt sorry for me and kindly let me register anyway. WHAT! Well, it looks like the universe was not being so generous after all. The next few minutes getting organised with wetsuits and tags and the mandatory nervous bathroom stop are a bit of a blur.

As I walked cautiously down the sandy path, I was terrified of what lay just beyond the tree-covered sand dunes. I wanted to cry when I saw the treacherous rips, waves, and unkind conditions. But standing in silence amongst the other swimmers, there was one thing that just begged to be acknowledged. The most magnificent golden sunrise was just beyond the island, which beamed back at the 100s of participants on the beach.

I knew then that I had to give it a go. If I could not get past the waves, I would just return to land. As I made my final preparations, I noticed one of the other swimmers standing next to me, still dressed. "You are swimming, aren't you?" I said. I reassured her that even though I was super nervous, I would give it a go and convinced her that she would regret it if she didn't. We agreed to go together.

As the 90 women stood on the edge of the beach facing the breaking waves and intense conditions, I felt comforted that I was not the only one but also damn fearful of not being able to do this. The whistle blew, and we all went running into the water. Just as I dived under my first wave, another came, and another. Diving deep under the white water, holding my breath until I could resurface again. A massive set of waves just happened to appear from nowhere, but the ocean is unpredictable like that. With waves and women everywhere, I didn't really have much time to panic. My body was purely in survival mode, and the only safe thing to do was keep swimming forward and diving under waves. The power of each waving pushing me back a few metres, forcing me to swim even stronger.

After what seemed like forever, myself and all the other women surrounding me, and I managed to get past the break and into the open water. However, it was still choppy and full of big swell. Like every other swim race I have been in before, it did not take long before everyone else was way ahead. And a group of stragglers, including me, brought up the rear.

As I composed myself a bit, I kept looking up at the island, which now looked like it was miles away. Due to the powerful sunrise, it was almost impossible to see the coloured buoys we were supposed to aim for. The water was murky and brown. It was rough and trying to see ahead was almost impossible. When swimming in rough water, you swallow a lot of water, and the taste of this salty brown ocean was anything but pleasant. All I could do was just keep swimming, but the island didn't seem to be getting much closer.

At one point, I looked up and saw a large group of swimmers heading to the southern side of the island. Still, I was sure I could see the purple buoys and water safety rescue boards further to the north. It is moments like this, you must make decisions on your own and trust your own intuition. I kept heading toward the north. After about another 15min I saw the big group of swimmers take a sharp left and head back in the correct direction.

I was finally starting to get closer to the island, but I didn't like what I could see, massive, big surf waves. My heart was racing as I imagined myself being smashed by the surf, and maybe I would drown. I figured at this point, if I had to swim further around the island to miss the waves, then that was what I was going to do. By the time I got close to the island, there were not many other swimmers, and I was in the back. Reaching the island was a huge achievement, and I took my time looking at the incredible cliff face and rock formations. I had no idea what to expect on this swim, and the island itself was bigger than I had imagined.

At this point, I felt excited that all I had to do was swim around the back and then head back to shore. It was all downhill from there. But it was a much longer distance than I imagined, and I was in the water for at least one hour before I got around the island. I was starting to feel tired, and each stroke of my arm was getting slower. All the salty water I had drunk was starting to make me feel a bit nauseous. To add to my disappointment, the water had been so murky the entire time that even if 100 turtles swam below me, I would not have seen a thing.

There was another lady just ahead of me as we came around the southern side of the island. There was plenty of water safety now, just keeping an eye on us and probably wishing we were a bit quicker. I was officially in last place. Usually, that would have stressed me out, but I was not phased because I knew I would complete my mission; all I had to do was swim back to shore. I was a bit surprised to see about twenty surfers catching massive waves just to my right but luckily, I was also too exhausted at this stage to care. All I wanted was to get back to shore.

What I expected to be the easiest part was now becoming the hardest. I had been swimming for over an hour, and the beach was not getting any closer. Or so it appeared. I kept putting one arm in front of the other, but I was definitely starting to get tired and over it. The other lady who was just ahead started to swim left, and most of the water safety followed her. I was left pretty much by myself. I was beginning to get frustrated at not getting closer. The neck of my wetsuit had started to rub on my skin. Even in the water, I could feel the raw burning of my skin each time I took a breath. I could see the red finish arch in the distance, but it was still so far away. Around this time, I came close to giving up, putting up my hand, and getting a lift back to shore. I had technically swum around the island. I had been swimming now for about 90 cleverly placed pockets minutes, and I do think I was starting to get a bit delirious. Maybe the beach was just a mirage?

But as I got even closer, it suddenly dawned on me that I would achieve this. I was going to make land after swimming around the island. Then it struck me that I still had to get through the surf. And during the time I had been swimming, the shore break had got much rougher. My exhilaration at completing this adventure turned back to panic again. As I calculated in my head what to do, I could not help smiling to think that Caroline, the non-swimmer, had done the impossible.

All she had to do now was not die of exhaustion getting through the surf. Using all my surf knowledge, I decided that the safest place for me to go was through the rip. It would be tougher energy-wise, but there were no big surfing waves to smash and drown me. I could barely swim at this stage. I was so fatigued, and I lost my swim cap as I got pounded by the waves pushing me into shore. I emerged out of the murky, messy surf to drag myself up the beach and through the finish chute. I smiled.

My biggest problem now is I must do it again because the brochure said I would see turtles!

I have not always been this courageous. In fact, for most of my life, I would say I was the complete opposite. Fearful and full of self-loathing. Childhood sexual abuse and over twenty years of addiction and depression have led to my life being a rollercoaster of self-sabotage and dysfunctional behaviour. My underlying fears and limiting beliefs were always setting me up for failure on every occasion.

In 2009, at the lowest of lows, I sought help to overcome my increasingly unhealthy alcohol addiction. With a six-pack of Black Ice Vodka in hand, I drove to my drug and alcohol counsellor, and within days I was detoxing on Valium prior to a six-month stint in residential rehab. It was from here my journey of courage would transform my life. Twelve years of sobriety have passed since that fateful drive, and I now lead a successful life. Fulfilling my passions of becoming a Life Coach, award-winning business owner and national athlete.

DISCLAIMER: The past twelve years have been anything but easy! In fact, my experiences of workplace bullying, failed relationships, mental illness, and the deaths of close family members have brought me to my knees on several occasions. Luckily, however, these experiences have also created resilience and courage.

It is my *Four Pillars Of Courage* that I want to share with you now.

The Four Pillars of Courage

Courage is defined as the "mental or moral strength to venture, persevere, and withstand danger, fear, or difficulty". (Merriam-Webster, 2021). After I got sober and faced many challenges, especially concerning my mental health, I began to understand what courage really means. Additionally, I could identify that I had shown incredible courage even through my 30 years of childhood sexual abuse and subsequent addiction. By reflecting on my life experiences, it became possible during my sobriety to integrate courage into my everyday life by following the following Four Pillars.

1. Confident

To be confident is to believe in yourself. Too often, people confuse ego and confidence. Ego is often exhibited when people use outside attributes of status, position, accomplishments, and physical characteristics to become more powerful and command the attention of others.

True confidence, however, comes from within. Having the ability to trust yourself no matter what the outside circumstances are. It was not until many years after getting sober that I replaced my previous self-hatred with self-esteem. My confidence was not created overnight but a journey of many factors, including getting mentors and coaches that positively influenced my life and a focus on wellness through a mind and body connection.

2. Candid

Say what you mean and do what you say! It is this simple, candid attitude that allowed me to gain respect amongst others and to stand up for what is important to me. Being candid is vital to being authentic.

In a world where people are being seduced daily by slick marketing campaigns praying on their fears and promising the world, be the person who has the courage to walk the talk. If you want someone to getting healthier, work on your own health.

If you want someone to reach goals, make sure you are hitting yours. Speaking out candidly about workplace bullying and harassment has been one of my most significant challenges in the past eight years. To stand in your truth requires courage, especially if your message threatens someone else abuse of power. I can say that despite the challenges or the hate I have endured by speaking out, being congruent with my beliefs and values has empowered me in so many positive ways.

Over time, the emotional challenges of being candid are reduced as we become more aligned with who we are and less concerned about what others think.

3. Consistent

My golden rule for courage and resilience is to chip away. As an impatient Aries, I used to think everything had to be changed or achieved instantaneously. A common theme in addiction is instant gratification. In our current fast-paced consumer society, this needs to have everything happen immediately harms our health and our success. What I now know is that perseverance and consistency are what brings actual results.

My success as a life coach and wellness hub founder did not come from 10xing my business in 3 weeks. It came from sustainability building a company that I could be proud of and has my client success at the core of my operations. In 2018 I set off to climb Everest Base Camp with my son.

I cannot think of a better example of being consistent every day to reach your goals. You cannot move fast because the oxygen saturation is so low, there are no quicker paths, and the conditions get increasingly challenging every day. It was a matter of putting one foot in front of the other, however slowly. Over a period of 8 days, I had trekked 62 km and climbed 5364 m to one of the most incredible destinations in the world.

4. Compassionate

Having courage also requires having a desire to help others through kindness. Being compassionate toward others allows you to be courageous on behalf of others or show courage in a manner that respects others. Having the added motivation of helping others has given me the strength to continue and persevere despite any fear or difficulty that I may encounter. I passionately believe in advocating and empowering others who may not have a voice or the confidence to stand up for themselves. By showing courage in these situations, you also inspire courage in others to speak out. It is for this reason that I talk openly about my childhood sexual abuse and mental health. On many occasions, showing courage has meant encountering opposing views and beliefs. This is often when showing compassion is the vital difference. Respecting others for their opinions and acting compassionately does not dilute your courage in overcoming difficulties.

By following the Four Pillars of Courage, I have lived authentically and congruently while achieving any goal that I set for myself. For this reason, I have pursued my current passion of being a Life Coach empowering others to find the courage to live a fulfilling life.

My 1:1 coaching programs are designed to assist women to achieve their own version of success and happiness.

Caroline's Ten Top Tips For Success

1. Live Courageously

2. Be Brave

3. Take Risks

4. Laugh Lots

5. Health Is Not Found on A Scale

6. Be Kind

7. Comparison Is The Thief Of Joy

8. Be Authentically YOU

9. Age Ungracefully

10. Say Yes and Then Work It Out

ABOUT THE AUTHOR

CAROLINE BELLENGER

Caroline Bellenger is a passionate life coach, motivational speaker, and creator of 'Be the Impossible'. The recent winner of The Gold Coast Women of The Year Wellness Warrior Caroline epitomises the philosophy of overcoming trauma through wellness and courage. From childhood sexual abuse to over twenty years of addiction and mental health issues, Caroline got sober in 2009. Since then, Caroline has achieved incredible success in life and business.

A few of her remarkable achievements include representing Australia in Triathlon at 50, climbing to Everest Base Camp, and going back to university in her 40s. After a successful corporate career ended through workplace bullying at the age of 48, she took back her life by becoming a successful entrepreneur with several businesses. These include a thriving fitness studio and life coaching business. Achieving entrepreneurial success over a few years is a testament to her courage and determination to not allow her past or age to define her future.

During her 12-year transition from self-hatred to self-esteem, Caroline created a powerful toolbox of strategies to overcome the many challenges and obstacles she faced. At the heart of her transformation was the ability to grow and move forward with courage, humour, and hope.

She credits much of her success to incorporating both exercise and a positive mindset into everyday practice. Caroline is passionate about inspiring women to reach their dreams. Caroline emphatically believes that if she can overcome significant life obstacles, then any woman given support and encouragement can achieve the impossible. This is why Caroline has dedicated her life to empowering other women through inspirational keynotes, coaching programs, and online education. Through all her social media channels, she raises awareness of childhood sexual abuse and mental health stigma.

Her life purpose is to help women find fulfilment and success by living courageously.

COACHING PROGRAMMES

1:1 Heal from Childhood Sexual Abuse in 6 Weeks
Her signature program is designed to help women who are still impacted by childhood trauma from childhood sexual abuse find the courage to overcome limiting self-beliefs and create a life full of happiness and success. This six-week coaching program includes 1:1 Coaching sessions, a private Facebook group and a six-week online course, The Self-Esteem Creator.

1:1 How to Reclaim Your Life In 12 Weeks
This 1:1 Coaching program is for all women who lack the courage to follow their dreams. Caroline will support and encourage you using her own Four Pillars of Courage Strategy to achieve everything you dreamed of, but thought was impossible.

This coaching package includes 1:1 coaching session, a private Facebook group, email support and access to the Be the Impossible Goal Setting Course.

BONUSES

Free Meditation – Trauma Healing Meditation

Please visit the website www.carolinebellenger.com to download this free meditation by Caroline that helps create agency regarding your experience of childhood sexual abuse.

Online Courses

The "Be the Impossible" series of online courses can be purchased separately. Please visit the website www.carolinebellenger.com to see all the current and upcoming courses.

- Goal Setting

- The Self-Esteem Creator

SPEAKING AND WORKSHOP EVENTS

Caroline is available for speaking and workshop events. Having won awards for her inspirational achievements and award-winning businesses, Caroline has spoken at various global events on a range of topics. Her inspirational messages of hope and courage are always authentic and raw.

Whether motivating a team or inspiring a room, Caroline under- stands how to engage with participants with a realness that resonates and influences change. The following is a list of her most popular topics; however, with a life rich in experiences, please contact her to see what would be best for your event or workplace.

1. Building Resilience
2. Four Pillars of Courage
3. Healing from Child Sexual Abuse
4. From Self-Hatred to Self-Esteem
5. Maximising Your Life by Minimising Your Drinking
6. The Secrets of Wellness

Connect with Caroline at:

Caroline Bellenger: 0466 372 211 (mobile)

Life Coach, Author, Global Speaker, Be The Impossible Founder

2021 Gold Coast Woman of The Year Wellness Warrior

Award-Winning Entrepreneur

Email: betheimpossible@carolinebellenger.com

www.carolinebellenger.com

- facebook.com/carolinebellengerofficial
- instagram.com/carolinebellengerofficial
- linkedin.com/in/caroline-bellenger

2
COLLABORATIVE PROSPERITY

by ANDREA PUTTING

STORIES of life are like a box of chocolates. It is filled with an assortment of different flavours and colours. We don't know if the one we select will be a favourite or one that we just want to spit out. Yet, when we bring them all together and share them with others, they create a beautiful selection of richness for all to enjoy. My stories are like this. Some of them are sweet and delicious, and others are hard to swallow. However, all of them have led to a greater appreciation of the box of chocolates that I now share.

Sitting on the hard wooden floor in my home study, my head between my hands, I felt my world caving in around me. It was all too hard. I had closed the door to my family. A rare moment that I could spend studying. However, the stresses of life were getting too much. I couldn't think. I could hardly put two words together. How on earth am I going to get this nutrition assignment done?

From my study window, I can see the driveway. There he was, my husband, a familiar sight chamois in his hands, bucket at his feet and busy washing the cars. His green Camry and my burgundy Magna, glistening in the sunshine. They were always spotless. Hardly his dream cars, however, he kept them immaculate. The bitterness and resentment were rising as I watched. "He spends more time with the cars than he does with me," I thought. I didn't realise then that this was his mindfulness activity and an essential escape from his overwhelming world.

I could hear my children playing outside in the afternoon sun. My son, aged 11, and my daughter, 9, loved a game of backyard cricket. Our bush-setting home gave them room to play and explore, and I was grateful. I was also thankful that I could spend most of their out-of-school hours with them. They were my priority.

During this time, my husband had just started on a new career path. He was fortunate to be taken under the wing by a family friend. They could see his potential to take his career to a higher level than that of an electrician. He was also ready for a more significant challenge and opportunity to provide for his family.

After a couple of years of mentoring, my husband was ready. Our friend, his mentor, was stepping out of the field for retirement. My husband was ready to step into the role. His first job was not for the faint-hearted. It was a significant construction job, the biggest of the time in Melbourne, where we live. This would cement him as a leading expert in his field of designing emergency power systems. However, it was a massive job with enormous demands. He was working 80 hours a week. In 1996, the options of working from home were not possible, so he would get up early to go to work and come home late to avoid the peak hour traffic.

It wasn't just his long hours of work that were straining the family. I was doing a double Advanced Diploma (equivalent to degrees, but not at that time recognised by the Australian Government), one in Naturopathy and one in Homoeopathy. My workload was enormous, and I felt that I had no support outside of me. As I sat on the floor on this day, I wondered, "if we separated, would people then help me?" My extended family were all busy with their own lives and didn't need my burdens. Who was there to support me as I felt my life falling apart?

Through this time, I referred to my husband as the "working zombie." He had no time for himself, no time for the children and no time for me. We were sitting on the side-lines, waiting for the crumbs of time to be scattered.

This is not just my story. Families everywhere struggle with this imbalance of work-life and family life. It pulls them apart literally and figuratively. It brings them to the point of despair. As pressures at work build up, it explodes into the family life. They take home with them all their stress. Their ability to cope with life is endangered. Their ability to share positively with their family is destroyed. **Their ability to contribute in the workplace suffers.** If we ignore how the job affects their lives, we choose low productivity, innovation, and profit.

When I completed my studies, going into business for myself was the obvious next step. After a few trials of how this can happen, my son suggested going on the internet with an online healing centre. It was all shiny and new in what I now call the dinosaur era of the internet. There was no Google, no Facebook, no PayPal, no WordPress. Only dial-up internet was available. I learned new languages, HTML, CGI, ASP, to build my website from scratch.

Over a few years, I built the business up. I had a following and an extensive database. My health articles could be found all over the internet and in print. As my business grew, I discovered my niche in a hard to come by product and my clientele grew.

With the help of my children, now teenagers, we packed hundreds of products every week and sent them all over Australia. Then one day, I stood in my dining room, looking at my table. It was covered in boxes ready to go out. A heaviness came over me. "Is this what I spent four and a half years study for to become a pack and send person?" It was hardly the vision that got me started.

What had happened to that vision, to that sense of purpose, that filled my being. The goals that had me in relentless pursuit, even in the early days, when there was no sales week after week. I did every- thing I could to make it happen. Now in this moment, where had it gone? Returning to my computer, I slumped in a heap. People depended on this service. However, right at that moment, it felt like I was being called to do something more significant in the world.

Divine providence stepped in, as my supplier was no longer able to supply. It was time to make some decisions. Do I find a new supplier? Do I find a new niche? Or do I get out altogether? A buyer stepped forward who could supply, and I opted to sell them the business.

Getting lost in the everyday "stuff" reduces business owners' opportunities to do what they are passionate about. Instead of following their visions and opening new doors, they are stuck just making sure ends meet, doing tasks that drain the life out of them. They need a team where everyone is doing what they love, then they all work at peak performance.

What would I do with my life now? "Why not get a job," the thought came. "Everyone else does it. It can't be that bad." My children were now grown and leaving the nest. It was time for me to explore the world and find something new. I was craving community, and I had worked on my own for long enough. What always excited me in my volunteer roles was how people come together and make something powerful happen. Now I wanted to be a part of a team that does something that matters in the world.

I found a job that suited my skills: leadership and management with natural health knowledge. The business was growing, and it had massive potential. Before me, the visions of what could be, excited me. It had the possibility of being a world leader, an authentic influence in the world. It soon became evident that these were not my visions to have as I was just the employee.

Over the next few years, my influence grew, as did the business. My work absorbed everything in my life. The growing team came to me as their manager and leader. They trusted in my calm and gentle ways to guide them in their day. Building relationships with clients, retailers and distributors gave me opportunities to gain experience. My work was varied from management to writing, to training, to developing, PR, website work, consulting with clients, you name it, I did it.

After a while, it started to crumble. The exhaustion of working and travelling long hours was hitting hard. However, my stubbornness was not letting me go. The cracks were not mine alone. Underlying the whole environment was the instability of the foundations. I clearly remember a train ride to work one day. Passengers packed in like sardines. I looked around at the expressionless faces. Everyone was dressed in black, except me, as if they were in mourning, as they go off to their soul-destroying job. Now that I had seen this, I couldn't unsee it.

It was everywhere. I could see it creeping into where I was working. People were disenchanted. I felt like we were asked to leave our souls at the door when we entered the workplace in the morning. Then at some stage, we'd forget to pick them up again at the end of the day. Everyone was getting lost in the pit of work.

What happened here is happening in workplaces everywhere. Businesses can't operate long or effectively in this environment. The CEO's and management feel like they are continually putting out fires. They have no energy left for development and growth. When everyone is disconnected from the core of who they are, not working in the way that makes them feel alive, discontentment is the result. Unless this problem is addressed, a toxic workplace will develop. Unhealthy competitiveness, people working in silos and bullying starts to creep in. No one wants to work here.

It was a Friday evening around 5:15 pm. I was walking to the train station to go home. The boom gates came down; the lights were flashing and dinging. I looked up. Speeding towards me was the express train. As it came close, out of nowhere was the thought, "It would be so easy to step in front of the train." Whoa! That hit me hard. I took a step back. This is not who I am. I don't think like that. How low has my whole life become to get to this point?

Right now, at this moment, I knew I had to leave. The feelings of worthlessness engulfed me. It was no longer where I belonged. I had lost interest. I was not expressing my best in this place, and something greater was calling me.

I spent some time healing and reflecting. Now I had three completely different perspectives on the working world.

- The difficulties and struggles as parents work long hours with little time to give to their families.
- The everyday grind that engulfs business owners and extinguishes their precious passion and vision.
- The dysfunction contributing to employees' disengagement, which burns them out and leaves them in pieces.

What were the gems that I could piece together from all of this?

While looking deeply at this, an event happened that opened **new ideas and visions of what could transform the lives of everyday workplaces** over the following few years.

On 15 December 2015, a gunman walked into the Lindt Chocolate Café in Sydney, taking the employees and patrons hostage. He claimed to be doing this in the name of Allah. Sadly, it culminated with two innocent people and the gunman passing away. In the after- math, it was feared that retaliation would be directed towards the Muslim community. Instead, there was an outpouring of love and acceptance. Social Media was filled with #Iwillridewithyou, offering Muslims to ride public transport with them to ensure they made it to their destinations safely.

I was deeply touched by this and inspired to start *Chocolate and Coffee* Day for Religious Harmony 12 months later. It is a simple concept. Reach out to someone different from you and share in the simple pleasures of life, chocolate, coffee, and conversation. When we do, we break down the barriers that divide the community.

People took to the idea and joined in as it gave them a sense that they could make a difference in the lives of others. *Chocolate and Coffee* Day has been shared every year since then, anywhere where people gather in many ways: Homes, schools, workplaces, community centres, places of worship, retirements villages and cafes.

The inevitable question came, why is it *Chocolate and Coffee* Day? We need this at other times too. As a result, *Chocolate and Coffee* Breaks emerged with new opportunities to become a community builder and a way for people to have open and honest conversations in a safe environment. Sharing chocolate and coffee has taken people from feeling isolated and lonely to finding a community where they feel safe and nurtured. When this happens, they want to contribute to the community that supports them.

All these stories danced around in my head. Nurturing communities of acceptance, belonging, and contribution appeared to be the answer. This was what was missing in the business settings I had experienced.

People didn't feel safe or have a sense of belonging. Without this, they live in survival mode and can't contribute to their fullest potential. As a result, neither does business.

The power of chocolate and coffee became evident. When people connect and learn each other's stories, they will work in more collaborative ways. Chocolate and coffee are now infused into everything I do. This was the beginning of developing **collaborative prosperity**.

Leaders Who Create a Sense of Belonging Will Change the World

We live in a divided world. The pandemic has separated us from each other. We have been in isolation, limited to travel only short distances. Unable to visit family and friends. Going to the workplace has been ruled out for most. The interactions that are vital for our mental health and survival have been non-existent. The business world is certainly not immune to this. It is suffering under the pressure of forced lockdowns and people working remotely.

Your team has not been able to function the way it used to. They struggle to be effective and efficient. Team members are distracted. Keeping them engaged and productive is a constant battle. They feel like they are trapped in silos, locked down in their own little world. Teamwork has gone out the window, along with productivity, innovation and profits. The connection they once thrived on has been snatched away from them.

For a business to move beyond the survival stage thrust upon them, their teams need to go beyond functioning. An effective team inter- acts with each other on more than a business level. Those that work at a high level exist with the personal interaction that gives them a sense of "I belong, and I am valued." Because of this, they want to make a difference in this place. When a community is present, team members are compelled to give their all. When they give their all, your business or company will excel and become a true authentic influence in the world.

How can you bring your people back together to work as a team? How can you get them to be all working on the same page? It can seem like an impossible task, especially where in some cases, being in the same place, at the same time, still doesn't happen. When every- thing feels like it is falling around you, how do you get to a collaboration stage where all can prosper?

Even if things could go back to the way they were, pre-pandemic, there would still be work to do to create an environment where team members all play full in. Times have changed, and a new approach to teamwork is required.

What people seek, and need more than ever, is what has been ripped away from them, connection. You may think it is not my role as a CEO or business owner to provide this. However, without a connected team, you cannot reach the fullest potential of your business. People will not work at their highest potential if they do not have a sense of connectedness with their colleagues and the workplace community.

According to a study on Global Work Connectivity, when people have workplace friendships, they are more engaged and committed to their job. They are more loyal to the business. They work more effectively together. They watch out for each other; they work together as a team and want their friends to succeed as much as themselves. 60% of those surveyed also said that they are less likely to leave when they have friends in the workplace. They stay for the community spirit. With only brief Zoom connections for meetings, the power of connectivity at work was lost.

In this new world, it will take something more significant than just working at the same place at the same time to survive and thrive greater than before. It's going to take everyone being on the same page. Ready, willing, and able to co-create. Whenever there is change or upheaval in any way, getting your team on the same page will require creating a new page where everyone gets involved. It will take **collaborative prosperity** - a future where everyone thrives. More significant, bolder and more inspirational visions of what can be will then be revealed.

Psychological safety is everyone's most basic need. If someone doesn't feel safe in the work environment, they won't be 100% present and will be more inclined to be disengaged and disruptive. When individuals all share a sense of community within the business, physical and psychological safety is high. This results in them being willing to experiment, take on new tasks, speak up when needed, share new ideas, and come together to collaborate.

But how do you rebuild your teams, so they are stronger and better than before? How can you reconnect your teams with each other to re-create their lives and your business?

You need to take your team from being functional to dynamic, thriving together through collaborative prosperity. In a study, 96% of executives cited lack of collaboration of ineffective communications as the cause of workplace failures. There is nothing more important in business than having a team that communicates effectively and collaborates. When you do, then everything runs more smoothly, and the company prospers.

When the environment encourages people to collaborate rather than compete, they go from working on their own individual agendas into a team working towards one vision. Creating a sense of community within your business is the start of **collaborative prosperity**.

It is Time to Change the Way Teams Work

What is **collaborative prosperity**? In basic terms, this means creating win-win-win situations. It is co-creating the future that we all want to have and creating a working environment where all grow and prosper.

To develop collaborative prosperity in any workplace, there are 5C's that need to be developed.

- Communication
- Collaboration
- Consultation
- Co-creation
- Commitment

The central key to all this is **communication**.

When you have a *Chocolate and Coffee* workshop with me, your team will come together and connect rebuilding and strengthening those lost connections or making new ones. In these fun and interactive sessions, they share in the delights of chocolate and coffee. The sweet aromas blending together create an environment where everyone feels safe and comfortable. As sharing together over "coffee" is some- thing we all do, there is a sense of familiarity that allows the flow of the conversation.

Chocolate and Coffee is an extraordinary communication tool that helps people to connect and reconnect at deeper levels. There's something special about those moments. A cuppa in our hands calms and relaxes us. Then we share chocolate—that soothing, delicious, seductive feeling of the chocolate melting in your mouth. It has all those delightful endorphins and dopamine, our feel-good hormones. It helps to open us up to each other to connect and communicate while unlocking our creativity.

Having a *Chocolate and Coffee* session creates a safe environment where team members can start to establish important trust amongst their peers. They share stories that they may have never shared before with work colleagues. Not because they didn't want to share, but because they didn't think anyone was interested.

For *Chocolate and Coffee* Day, I created a pack of conversation starter cards that helps people get to know each other. These are not the usual questions you ask when you meet somebody. "Hello, how are you? What do you do?" But deeply personal questions that aren't invasive. Questions that help people get to know who the other person is. They are perfect to start the process of teams reconnecting. This also allows them to find some commonality between them. They open up into areas they haven't explored together before.

Each person starts to feel that who they are and what they bring to the table is important. When they have been acknowledged as an individual, they can work together in a team more effectively. This is the start of co-creating a team that cares about each other and the work that they do.

Communication can make or break a business. If anyone in a team doesn't feel comfortable or safe communicating with another team member, the whole team can suffer. Everyone needs to feel a personal connection and that they can participate as a valued team member. The power of this is vital in creating psychological safety that is required for teams to work at optimal levels together.

Listening to the stories of team members can open up new avenues to explore. Activities that reveal why people work in this company and what they love about being here started to unravel. Through the exercises and sharing experience, they begin to discover shared values and experiences that will build community and help grow the business. They start to understand each other and gain new insights into the importance of this business and community to them.

When you create a community within a business, you remove limitations from your growth potential. When your team feel nurtured, they are empowered to embrace their own potential. In this, the company finds its ultimate impact.

Working with people as a community, rather than as silos in isolation of each other, starts to break down the barriers to where real success can unfold. The team experience gives us a glimpse of something greater that can be accomplished if we put aside our own agendas and work together. Here we can integrate our individual ideas, give, and receive feedback, be supported, and create new and better cooperative ideas. When these all pull together as a team, you start to have your authentic influence.

Collaborative prosperity unlocks the full potential of people. When they can express themselves and do what they do best and enjoy doing, they are naturally more collaborative in their approach.

A *Chocolate and Coffee* workshop in your company is the beginning of creating a sense of community in your business. When you do, everyone has the same goal, the same purpose. They share the same direction and are all emotionally involved in the outcome. People want to grow to help make this happen, and they now have something to believe in.

When teams start to function with purpose and desire to make a difference, magic happens. Here is where new visions for what can be, begins to emerge. Where they can grow as a community, the future starts to unfold. Add to this the beauty of each person feeling a sense of ownership in new projects. More significant commitment begins to flourish as a whole.

We are all on the endless quest to find something that will make us feel good and give us a sense of purpose and feeling that we are making a difference. When a business or organisation offers this to their employees and consumers, it is on a path to winning.

Collaboration is something we all need to be able to do to survive, develop and grow. There is no better way to do this than sitting down with someone over chocolate and coffee and allowing the conversation to flow.

Community is the heartbeat of your organisation. When you nurture community within your company, you will go beyond your greatest dreams.

> *Sometimes you come across great leaders who have natural abilities but no real understanding of how they do it, so cannot share the why, how, what, when or who. Andrea Putting is a great leader with innate talents that can explain how to become a great leader yourself. I have now worked in a voluntary role with her for over 3 years and know that her guidance has made a huge difference to who I am today. I recommend that you connect with her ideas and passion for making a difference in communities for all of us."*
> *—**Leigh-Anne Sharland, Founder of Building Your Mindset Muscle and Executive Advisor in Change.***

In chocolate, I have found a great friend and ally that consistently leads the way. It opens doors and brings people together to allow building connections by breaking down the barriers that may prevent them from working together effectively and efficiently. For teams to become successful, this is always the place to start.

Chocolate and Coffee Breaks has been growing around the world. Along with it has my opportunities to speak and facilitate workshops internationally. In 2018, I found myself sitting in my home office, presenting a seminar to a Bank in India. At the time, conducting virtual and hybrid events was not the norm. By the time Covid hit, I was already on the ball, and I could see what was possible.

Since then, I have had the delight and privilege of presenting *Chocolate and Coffee* workshops throughout Australia and Internationally, in person and virtually. These experiences have drawn people together to enhance their connectedness at conferences, retreats, and corporate settings. The importance of people connecting one-on-one at events has often been overlooked since the world went virtual. Adding a *Chocolate and Coffee* Break has allowed participants to have heartfelt conversations with others, enhancing their overall experience.

The potential goes further with opportunities to bring new teams together as they prepare to start a new project. It also can be integrated throughout the project to open into Brew Sessions - co-creative coaching sessions, where new ideas and solutions can be found.

Andrea's Ten Top Tips for Growing Collaborative Prosperity in Your Organisation

- Schedule in regular *Chocolate and Coffee* Breaks when people can connect on an informal level. This allows for the vital building of connections, developing a culture of open and honest conversation creating a sustainable and prosperous team.

- Set the example of receiving feedback in your organisation with gratitude. When you are open to receiving it, your team are more likely to respond likewise.

- Take time to listen to your people. Not just on the surface level. Understanding who they are, where they are coming from, and how they think will guide you in how to bring out the best in them and build trust between you.

- Encourage team members to talk through their problems with each other rather than struggling alone.

- Consult with all relevant team members to develop solutions. They are the ones living it and will have the best insights and ideas.

- Always look beyond the surface to discover what is happening at the core level.

- Work together to design projects, creating a unified vision. Doing this will build emotional buy-in from all team members, and they want the project to succeed, as it belongs to all.

- Introduce "Brew Sessions", where teams come together to stay updated on a project and allow new ideas to brew on how to move forward.

- Make sure everyone is on the same page by regularly revisiting your values, mission, and vision with your team. Circumstances change, and team members come and go; this alters the way everything works.

- Ensure you have the right people doing the right jobs at the right time. This is where you make the difference and co- create Collaborative Prosperity.

ABOUT THE AUTHOR

ANDREA PUTTING

"Andrea Putting is a heartfelt, compassionate and strategic thinker who has developed a wonderful concept that acknowledges diversity as a key element of building community. She uses chocolate and coffee to bring people together to engage and get to know each other."
—***Leo Coco, Project Management Authority - Success & Personal Development Coach***

As an International Speaker, Best-selling, Award winning Author and Trusted Advisor to Authentic Influencers, I will be honoured to work with you and your team to develop collaborative prosperity.

Speaking has always been a significant part of my life. I have been gifted with the ability to deliver a message that inspires the mind, touches the heart, and awakens the soul.

You can book me to speak at conferences, seminars, and for your workplace gatherings, in person or virtually.

My topics include:

Collaborative Prosperity – Growing Teams who Change the World

Compassionate Prosperity - When Success Is Not Enough

Compassionate Purpose – Discovering a Life of Fulfilment

The Chocolate and Coffee Way – Embracing Diversity in Community

Chocolate and Coffee Workshops are designed according to the needs of your organisation. We discover the current issues you need to address and where your vision is taking you through consultation. With this in mind, the workshop delivered to you and your team will give you a laser focus on your direction.

> *Andrea has the ability to help participants build a greater connection and understanding of each other. To appreciate their diversity. To discover new ways to nurture oneself, acknowledge giftedness, joys and inner strengths."*
> **—Helen McIlroy, workshop participant, Minister, Business Owner**

A do-it-yourself *Chocolate and Coffee* Workshop is available. While it will not be customised, your team will gain significant benefits from connecting together.

Working with me is all about bringing teams together in a way that permits each individual to step up into their personal calling. They are empowered to discover their strengths and then use them to support the goals of the team.

Teams become stronger and more committed to each other and their work. Beyond chocolate and coffee, my methodology is based on work used worldwide by universities, governments, corporations, businesses, community groups, and individuals to solve problems and initiate new projects.

> *When the heartbeat of a business and organisation is lost, the numbers will quickly portray that same story. Andrea Putting has transcended her lived experiences in the work place. Add to this her years of research and service to community and she is indeed an Authentic Influencer. This is a time of great responsibility for CEO's and Business Leaders to nurture their community. I highly recommend you invite Andrea as your Trusted Advisor to strengthen the heartbeat of your organisation / business. With her eloquent guidance, you can create and nurture your teams and watch them and your numbers soar."*
> —**Heather Joy Bassett, Business Life Strategist**

To create the world, we all want to live in, we need great leaders. The Authentic Influencers of this world are the leaders who support, nurture, and empower their teams. They will change the world together through **collaborative prosperity**.

Connect with Andrea at:

Email: queens@andreaputting.com

www.AndreaPutting.com

www.SocialMissionRevolution.com

www.ChocolateandCoffeeBreaks.com

YouTube: https://www.youtube.com/c/AndreaPutting

facebook.com/AndreaPuttingSpeaker

instagram.com/AndreaPutting

linkedin.com/in/AndreaPutting

3

GIRL FINDS HER PURPOSE AND SOUL GRIT

by LARA ZELENKA

AT what point do you stand up and say enough! Enough of their conditioning. Enough of them trying to make and mould you into what they think I we as girls, young women and women are "meant to be" whether it be your parents, the system, teachers or even yourself through some sort of warped lens that has got so confused and so far away from the real reason and the true purpose you were put on this earth and all you were sent here to achieve and do and to be your true brilliant self.

Whether the conditioning involved someone telling you, you had puppy fat, "don't wear red lipstick as only those kinds of women wear red lipstick," "don't wear that, as everyone can see what you had for breakfast." Huh! "Don't wash your hair when you have your period," "say another Hail Mary instead of listening to that screeching cockatoo Jimmy Barnes!"

Is it any wonder, we as women want to escape as little girls and even as big girls, escape to safe hide away, where we can be safe, be seen, be heard, be felt and be witnessed for who we want to truly be and who we can begin to practice who we want to be to the outside noisy, crazy, cruel world that is often trying to make us everything we don't want to be or simply go somewhere to dress up in our very own grown- ups bedroom (*do you remember escaping to your teenage sanctuary where you listened to music, dreamed your very own dreams and rebelled*) and play and explore and become the Boudoir Babe we want to be, feeling that feeling of total confidence and safety in our body, mind and SOUL!

As a recovering people pleaser, you know… the person who says yes to doing something before the requester has even asked most of the time - yep that was me! Super-Woman, I used to feel like I might of wore my undies on the outside and had cape on to, I was a bloody perfectionist, never made a mistake, in fact, I would not allow myself to and forbade it in fact, ruled my-self with an iron fist, I was never 1 minute late to anything and always said yes to absolutely everything that was requested of me and often more. This is just what we women good girls -conditioned to within an inch of their life do right? WRONG!

I can distinctly remember the rush and driving around getting between work sites at the time, we were deep in preparation for the audit and failing just was not an option. The stress of passing this audit at any cost was immense. On this particular day, I had been asked to deliver some training to a new site Manager. On the way to the site, I began to feel a little shaky and thought…. It might be that I am just tired, I then began to have trouble swallowing and was afraid to swallow for fear of choking. What was happening here, I asked myself? I pulled over for a minute, got myself together and began my journey again.

In the ensuing weeks the pressure around this audit was purely and simply palpable, I was running quite literally between four jobs to ensure our documents ship shape and we were looking okay ready for audit day, during this time, I was feeling very flat, not sleeping, that feeling of being afraid to swallow kept continuing and I was exhausted, physically, mentally, and most of emotionally. I was very shaky, super hyper vigilant and on guard and very teary. We passed audit by 1 point and what should have been sheer relief at this point wasn't for me, I was feeling constantly on edge, afraid of swallowing, not sleeping, finding it hard to focus and I can clearly remember R U OK Day 2019 just wanting to fall in in a heap and crumble.

That Saturday morning, I was doing our weekly grocery shop as usual, I was standing there deciding what to pick out for my husband's smoko for the following week and I began to shake uncontrollably, feeling very hot and like everything was closing in on me. I remember thinking, do I call for help, do I call Paul, do I leave the shopping? Should I call an ambulance? Everything in Coles was spinning, it was like I was in a horror movie or some weird LSD situation (not that I know what that is).

I mustered up enough mental cognizance to get around the shop, holding onto the shopping trolley while deeply breathing in through my nose and out though my mouth. My knuckles were white, that's how tight I was holding onto the shopping trolley. I was even leaning on it and the shelves at one point to steady myself. I managed to get through the cash register and home to unpack the shopping, showering, and calling Paul to come home. I sat on the lounge, called the Doctor's surgery, and waited.

Paul steadied me as we shuffled into the Surgery. I remember feeling violently ill. The doctor took my BP that was extremely high and gave me a few days off work. I went back to work and struggled on. After that I had days off here and there, travelling backwards and forwards to the surgery. I was struggling. Every time I moved my body felt heavy, I was doing a double take and my head felt like cotton wool. I was frightened day in day out, while trying to keep the mask of 'I'm okay' both at work and socially. Meanwhile completely falling apart every afternoon when I got home. My body literally felt like it was buried in concrete. It was SO surreal.

There was a day I woke up and I felt shocking, I was shaking, crying, and wanted to vomit. I couldn't even drive to work. I called my dad, and he took me in. I was there only a little while when I began to feel very unwell and began to cry and just knew I owed it to myself to let the mask melt away. I knew I could not keep on living like this.

My boss drove me home, I called my doctor's surgery and crawled under a heavy blanket on the lounge and that was my safe place for the next four weeks, while I navigated my new life. I called Paul and my Dad they came to my side straight away.

We called the doctors. By this time, he had a prescription for Valium ready for me to fill along with a medical certificate for a week off work and an instruction to see him in one week. Paul took the week off with me, I can remember my body feeling so very much like it had never felt before, my head was all over the place, and I was feeling very alone and frightened even with the support of my family and friends. I was so blessed to have this. I laid on the lounge under the protection of that heavy blanket for three days straight.

I lasted on the Valium two nights and just could not cope with how it made me feel, it was like I was on another sphere somewhere. Paul asked me if I could face getting out of the house to go clothes shopping with him to use a voucher he had, I was so frightened and super weary, but I did it sticking beside my best friend and life partner the whole time.

Thinking about it ... and with the benefit of hindsight, it was the best thing he could have probably ever done. I have never felt so bloody horrendous but proud of myself at the same time, even though I was squeezing my poor husband's hand so tight, and we did it together. It was the very first step/s of me beating whatever the heck this thing was.

The feelings and toll this disorder were having on my body was intense. My head felt like something was in there, buzzing around and the absolute feeling of dread and fear was so overwhelming. I can remember sitting at my desk at work before I chose to put myself first and surrender to the process and take the much-needed time I so deserved.

I was cajoling myself "C'mon Lara move your legs, move your arms and get up, type something, please God!"

Don't let anyone talk to me so I don't have to respond and can appear to be a normal functioning adult. Internally it was like I was walking with sandbags around my body, the heaviness and disorientation was awful. I needed to clutch onto a wall or any object close by, to steady myself as I passed by. This became part of my everyday existence.

I was so shaky from the effects of the Valium but knew I was safe with Paul and had taken the first steps out from under that blanket. Paul had taken that week off to be with me and made sure I was okay.

The following Monday Paul went back to work, and Dad took me to see my GP. He listened ever so caringly to me as I explained while crying, what had been happening to me the last week and prior. He took my BP. It was still very high, and my heart was racing. He held my hand ever so kindly and said Lara I believe you have PTSD! I said "What? Nuh... no way!"

That is what returning soldiers have, I know, I work around them day in day out! I do not get the right to have that. He repeated it again ever so slowly. He began to speak of a plan of medication, antidepressants, sleeping tablets and tablets to slow my poor old ticker down and a mental health plan, to see a psychologist. I was in denial right there and then and for a period of a few days. Was I in denial though or was I secretly relieved that this thing, this monster finally had a name or was that giving it a reality and an identity?

Again, I laid on the lounge under that safe blanket and watched garbage TV. By the third day, I was determined to prove him wrong. I went to the spare bedroom and began to put my work out clothes on, I remember saying to myself and thinking about all the reasons why I couldn't or shouldn't go and wander out there, into that scary big world. Then I remembered and told myself why I should.

I was dressed and so afraid. I laid back down on that bloody lounge again and then …. I got up off that bloody lounge and went for a walk in the sunshine of the early morning, and it felt good. It felt bloody good in fact.

From this day on I was still very reliant on my heavy blanket for protection almost to get me through every day and life still felt very surreal, however, I also knew I had literally taken my very first steps back to my new life living with PTSD. I needed to accept and embrace it, even though I was not a war veteran or fought a physical war overseas. I was fighting my very own war, that of my child-hood abuse, neglect, and terrible trauma that I had and continue to have every right to acknowledge, speak and grieve over. I should not and will no longer be silenced - it is my time to speak up!

This day was Day 1, but it was far from being the easiest. The days, weeks and months were paved with many twists, turns and learning curves for me.

I required a stress test on my heart, was referred to the dizziness clinic, for more medication and what they thought were vestibular migraines and Irlen Syndrome which I have recently found out is Right Angel Attack…. after two years.

I can't even count the number of mornings I would wake up feeling heavy like concrete, jumpy, lying-in bed, willing myself trying to get up and scared to do anything. I just knew that shaky feeling of overwhelm and not being able to cope with this monster that was called PTSD, would be there and join me as I wandered down the hallway to begin my new day. Don't even get me started about loud noises, music, too many people in a crowded place. Paul closing a door or a drawer too loudly.

I would just hold my ears and plead for it to all go away.

I can distinctly remember baulking at needing to take "all this" what seemed to be a mountain of medication, I would sit at the dining room table and just stare at the tablets and not want to take them for fear of what they may or may not or could or could not do to me. I would sit there at the table and stare at the tablets and say "Nuh! Not taking this rubbish!" Feeling so exhausted and frightened with this monster living in my body but feeling even more frightened of these chemicals. Crying and sobbing and Paul loving me through this bloody awful time. Paul would say quietly but firmly "C'mon baby take them."

Eventually, around three weeks or so later, the medication began to take affect and at each visit to my GP, he would adjust the dose, "increasing" my medication. I can remember being so filthy about needing to take medication, at one particular visit to my doctor and there were many, I said to him I am ticked about all this medication (I am feeling better - when can I start coming off this one and that one) as he as was still adding to get the dosage correct there for a period of time, one for the sleep, one for the head, one for the racing heart, one for the migraine one for the rising blood pressure. He looked at me and said, "it seems a lot, but there are people out there on double what you are taking." Hmm! I thought to myself!

For nearly a month I watched trashy TV and researched support services "out there" for women newly diagnosed with this debilitating mental illness, there is not a lot out there! My doctor informed me the statistics of women diagnosed within my age group, are remarkably high.

Wow! I SOH wanted to do something about this, however the time was just not right. My doctor asked me if I was to try to go back to work a few days a week, me being instantly replied with nun! If I am going back, I will go back full on or not at all, my job and employer don't do part time. I also knew secretly, I had to get back on with life or if I did not there and then I may fall into the lull of being at home "like this" forever.

The nearly two years that have ensued have seen me getting my medications right which are a big part of this journey, sourcing the right and seeing my psychologist regularly, a mountain of research and gaining support and skills required to start my own support service and movement for women named Boudoir Babe and am going to everything I can to provide support for that massive gap of need of support for women who also face going through this journey and the early days of diagnosis as it is bloody scary and lonely. You are loved, supported and not alone, you are a Boudoir Babe!

Through this journey I not only found myself I found my purpose in this life, but it has also been an epic, would I change anything, hammam! This ride has shaken me to my core quite literally, but my inner guidance and compass was there the whole time. I just needed to stop searching for external validation so much, tune into my own frequency, rid myself of the outside noise and static a bit more and vibe to my very own ebb and flow and believe.

From the time of the initial episode in the supermarket, to being diagnosed with PTSD; until the true levelling out of medication and feeling somewhat okay and not so shaky and adrenaline fuelled, it was quite the adventure and journey in itself.

The journey to embracing, healing, and living life now just as full as prior to this life changing event was twisting, turning, full of triumph, torment, and turmoil as lots of new journeys and roads in life often are right!

Jumpy does not begin to explain what I was feeling in my physical body, constantly in fight, flight or freeze. Every morning I would wake and almost force myself to get up like a frightened little child and sit at the side of our bed and will my body to get up and move for the day. I would make it as far as halfway down the hallway and just want to go back to bed, I just wanted to cry. I would muster up enough strength to put the jug on for a cuppa for Paul and I some mornings and sit on the lounge and just wish the world would go away pretty much.

On really bad mornings if Paul closed a kitchen cupboard or drawer I would jump through the roof. Most mornings I would have to go and lie back on the bed just to centre myself to cope with the day ahead.

For me to be able to return to work that break of nearly a month I couldn't drive at this point or for a very long time after that, my father said he would drive me so on the very first day I was due back at work, I remember sitting on the lounge after Paul went off to work, I was sitting there thinking "can I do this?" I was very shaky and scared and my head was buzzing, I was I also knew If I didn't make some sort steps back to reality and life as I knew It before all this happened I may never do so again.

It was right about now I was beginning to think my GP's option of returning to work part time was appealing. I talked and paced myself all the way through having a shower, getting ready and throughout having breakfast and before I knew it Dad was out the front like my knight in shining armour ready to take me to work.

It was around this time; I saw a Psychologist (I only saw this one once) but in the hour I spent with her she taught me a fair bit about the Parasympathetic nervous system. When I got to see her, I was breathing so shallow (from the chest) she was overly concerned as my blood pressure was sky high and my GP was still waiting for the Prazosin to kick in and altering it between 1mg and 5mg at this point. She asked me to slow my breathing down and I was like 'whatever,' I am sick of hearing people telling me to do this lady you can run and jump…. type of thing.

However, she then went on to draw and explain the Parasympathetic nervous system, it goes like this, the part of the involuntary nervous system that serves to slow the heart rate, increase intestinal and glandular activity, and relax the sphincter muscles. The Parasympathetic nervous system constitutes the automatic nervous system. Wow!!! I had two choices here, ignore her and keep on breathing shallow and growing even more anxious or listen to her and her instructions on breathing from my diaphragm correctly.

I chose to listen to her, and it began to feel a little bit better while there. All I could think at the time was…. What have I got to lose other than feeling a little bit better maybe? I went on to feel better by breathing deeper longer and began to reduce my anxiety. This better breathing and the Prazosin starting to level out made me feel a bit better.

I have always exercised, I kept walking and incorporated meditation into my daily routine. I had absolutely no clue how to do this or what I was doing, I trawled the internet for some time, and nothing resonated with me and then stumbled across this beautiful 10-minute meditation appeared, it was soft it, it soothed my frayed nerves and got me through those scratchy early days. Walking and plenty of fresh air cannot be over mentioned here, nor can connecting with friends and family who make you feel good about yourself and that don't criticise you or put you down.

I tried journaling, it just doesn't work for my needs, I know it does for others however what really does and just speaks to my heart and soul is oracle (not tarot) cards and from the very first day I returned to work I shuffled my cards that were work and the message was spot on for me and has been ever since through this journey as previously for me in my life.

I connect with my heart and soul ask/seek what it is I need to know today, shuffle my cards exactly thirteen times lay my cards of choice (I have a few Shah) either spread them to the left on the table with my right-hand side of my brain, this coming from the masculine energy field and left-hand side of my brain is the female energy field. I then spread my energy through all the cards while they are face down with both hands exactly and evenly, I then feel where I am drawn to in the pack and pick that exact card for a one-card spread or cards for a two-card or more spread etc.

Lipstick. Yup. Something as simple as putting on colour every day made me feel SO much better. I didn't necessarily feel like putting on a lot of other makeup, but I could manage a beautiful lippy. I simply can't and won't leave home without my colour lippy now.

Another factor that helped me on my healing journey is Vitamin D, yes good old-fashioned soaking up the rays of the day and moon- beams of the evening to. Bask in them where and where you can, they are natural and our grandmothers did not need to take supplements, but we do, there is a message around this.

Lots of sleep, self-pacing both at work and home are particularly important factors as are learning to say what you mean and mean what you say. Do not be afraid to say no! With no buts… or "do you mind?" when asked to do something that is going to compromise your mental, physical, and emotional health.

It feels strange when you have been a people pleaser and even a doormat most of your life but it does get easier with time and practice. And it more than okay to delegate tasks without the need for explanation why. When you feel tired, rest. No permission is required. Not even yours!

Be kind and gentle on yourself while you adjust to life with your cocktail of medications and know these may be in your life temporarily or more permanently, whatever the case maybe, it's all okay and you are going to be okay to, Source yourself an awesome medical and psychological team (this is not as easy as it sounds).

Lastly and the most importantly of all, finding your true north and the true YOU in all this. Not the mental health diagnosis, not all that is going on but the true essence of YOU, your soul, and the self-belief that you can and will get through this experience. This is what it is, an experience and you are reliving memories of past traumas that can't really hurt you any longer it's the ghosts that linger in your memory from those traumas that have come to visit you and that have been set off by a very stressful event.

Having a purpose, self-belief and self-love are often so underestimated but the trilogy that will pull you out of the darkest and deepest depths of despair so often, overcoming that old adversary self-doubt, which creeps up and builds and before you know it has taken over your life. Loving yourself and self-kindness and compassion is such a beautiful strength to have both inside and out and to have and know your purpose on this earth. That is the grandmaster key to the golden gates of life my beautiful friend, power, and purpose equals.

5 Morning Exercises

1. At the beginning of each and every day on this earth I take a big breath/sigh and say thank you to myself and the greater source that sent me here to do my work and I wear lipstick every day.

2. My mobile phone is constantly on silent mode, I control it, it does not control me! Much to the bewilderment of some people in my life. I check my phone on my terms and action what requires actioning equally on my terms not necessarily when it rings.

3. I commune with nature on the daily, I simply must absorb some sun rays or some moon rays, see the trees swaying, my favourite thing to listen to is the trees rustling on a very windy day and speaking to each other, but I must absorb some sort of nature.

4. I draw an Oracle (not tarot) card and it is always spot on for what is happening right there in that moment in my life.

5. Last and by no means least and probably most importantly is to move my body in some shape or form, be it walking, seeing the sun come up (what a magical and peaceful time of day zoning out and communing with nature) dancing crazily on my own (I don't care who's watching), yoga, whatever it is, I MUST move my body or I can feel the effects and they are not good, mentally, physically, emotionally, spiritually.

The Boudoir Babes Ten Top Tips to Business Success

1. Value Every Working Relationship

It's my experience that every person in an organisation deserves the same level of respect and that's exactly what they receive from me. Whether you're the cleaner or the CEO, I am the same person with both working relationships. I always find and try to think of some- thing to connect to people that I encounter, that is super important to them. I never want them feeling I've forgotten who they are or what their business stands for.

2. Leverage One of Your Greatest Resources - Your Current Network

Don't forget this gold nugget is already within your business toolkit. It's often forgotten, and this easy business hack returns impressive results. Do you know someone whose skill set lies in sales, marketing, or journalism? If so, it's time to dust off old relationships and make use of your network. Don't be afraid to reach out to those networks for help or call in an old favour to improve your business to improve your own business. People are looking for connections with other business owners they know, like and trust, so don't underestimate the power of your well-established networks.

3. Team - When only the Very Best Will Do *Only hire the very best!*

I am sure we've all heard this old cliche right? Easier said than done Sista! I've been there many times before and am still there. You can apply all the interviewing techniques in the world, and we have all heard the old "your employees are an extension of your routine." I've had the very best and the very worst and you know what? They're human beings, all having their own set of challenges they bring to you and your business. The best thing you can use is good old intuition, insight, gut feeling and common sense on which person sitting before you is going to help you lead your business towards success.

4. **Focus Your Time on What's Working**

Do not do something just because it's the trend and everyone else is doing it. Invest the time to find out what key performance areas are leading to growth within your business. Apply regular test, measure, and evaluation processes on projects. Know when something is not working and do not waste time procrastinating. A negative mindset will cause you to lose valuable resources such as your precious energy on this.

5. **Seek out Longer Term Benefits to Shorter Term Gratification and Success**

In today's fast paced, instant gratification and fast results world, people are looking for instant sales and instant success. Often grabbing at less labour-intensive small tasks that deliver quick results and make you feel good in the short term, a good old-fashioned rush of Dopamine, right? Try re-thinking and re-structuring to a more comprehensive long-term strategy that yields results for years to come. Take time to plan and make better use of your time on achieving long term sustainable results.

6. **Being Innovative**

Being a leader in a business is all about innovation, being creative and having the ability to understand the industry you provide a service to. It's also showing up as a provider who is bold, fresh, and above all present for the client and who embraces the challenges of business and makes them their ally and keeps showing up continuously regardless.

7. Have Integrity

People like to know they're in safe hands and that they're working with a business they can utterly trust. This goes beyond the ink drying on the paper on contract. My motto is "My word is my personal guarantee to you that I will do the right thing by you" I will always speak the truth especially when I have made a mistake. Be genuine, your clients will sniff in-genuine a mile off and be the best of the best, but you do need to be genuine, honest, and moral.

8. Establish a Strong Company Culture

I have found success in building and creating team culture and traditions. Building a successful business culture makes employees feel like part of your extended family and invites them into a sense of knowing they are appreciated, valued, and focus their skills on improving the business. It could be lunch at the club every Friday or team activities. It doesn't have to be huge and overwhelming it just needs to be enough to be sincere, loyal, and meaningful.

9. Make Sound Financial Decisions

Don't get caught up in what everyone else around you are doing. Don't get too caught up in what others are doing in their business similar to yours. Don't compare your worst day to someone's high- light reel. You don't really know where people's resources come from, they could be in debt to the bank or someone else to the eyeballs and not telling you. Live and grow your business within your means, don't compare yourself to others is the most important aspect here. You are you and they are who they are, and Business is bloody tough. No one goes into business to fail. Ultimately the buck literally starts, stops and everything in between with you as the business owner even when it can't be found to pay a bill.

10. Enjoy the Ride

You have gone into business for yourself, not by yourself…well you know what I mean right? This business is where you can showcase to the entire world the true essence of who YOU really are. Imagine the possibilities, wonderment, and joy you can bring to yourself, others, and industry, when you are in true embodied enlightenment of knowing who you truly are, doing what you want to do and working for yourself. You have the POWER and GENIUS ZONE within you to do this. NEVER FORGET THAT. And look after yourself first and foremost, the business needs you, the clients need you, you need YOU babe. To be completely successful in business you need to know when to retreat and rest and when to fire on all cylinders. You are a business owner not a miracle maker.

ABOUT THE AUTHOR

LARA ZELENKA

" I have been privileged to witness Lara break out of her cocoon, spread her wings and take flight. The healing and growth that Lara achieved in such a short amount of time is a testament to her willingness to do the internal work and face challenges head on.

Lara has helped me through some very challenging moments in my life by offering compassion, encouragement, and unconditional love. She has a way of seeing and accepting people that is rare in today's world and now she uses her knowledge, power and experience to fight for women who don't yet know how to do it for themselves."
—***Erica Kostiuk - Life and Relationship Coach***

" It has been and is an absolute pleasure working with Lara. She has a beautiful presence and way of holding space. You know that Lara will treasure your dreams and fight for them as much as you do. Knowing Lara is a gift that I am grateful for receiving in my life."
—***Carrie Adlington - Empowerment Coach***

Connect with Lara at:

- facebook.com/lara.zelenka
- instagram.com/lara_zelenka
- instagram.com/lara_portelli1106
- linkedin.com/in/lara-zelenka-743220163

4

MY MAGIC MIKE MOMENT

by TIFFANY DROGE

How Ginuwine's Pony and Spaghetti Bolognaise inspired my business.

FINALLY! I've found my calling, and it was staring me right in the face this whole time. How could I not see it! Gazing at my silhouette in the reflection of the mixing bowl, I had a light bulb moment. Shit, I need to dance again! The rush of pure joy filled my body as the music enveloped me. Removing all the stresses in the world at that very moment. I was free and happy.

Dancing, moving, thrusting, sweating, shaking it like no one was watching. Beats that you feel deep in your soul. Heart pounding with excitement at doing something sexy, feeling nervous that you might get found out because you can't keep up! The music explodes and it's your fave jam. Boom you're in!

Welcome to Shake It Mumma! The Sister's Dance Party!

The power women have to shake it, move it, and release that tension that they've been hanging onto, … is my true passion. I'm so pumped that I can give back to women who are in need of gifting themselves the precious time they deserve. This allows them to let loose and have a bit of crazy time as a supportive sisterhood tribe that's bursting with energy and excitement.

HOW MY VIBRANT ENERGETIC SISTERHOOD DANCE PARTY BECAME Shake It Mumma!

One Sunday afternoon I was starting to prepare dinner spaghetti bolognaise for my family. I was in my usual attire: loose singlet top, drop-crotch track pants (you never know when a dance party will happen, so always need to be prepared I say), hair up in a messy bun but tied up behind a purple bandanna. I felt the urge to pump up my tunes and shake it while I was cooking and knew my music was going to get highly inappropriate for young ears. I kicked my kids and husband Nath out of the house to play in the backyard. I desperately needed some time to myself! Dancing right now to my favourite music was better than washing my hair or any other luxury self-care I could think of. This was my precious moment. Music on…. volume up…. here I go!

I started chopping the onions and with each slice, I was moving my hips to the beat of Pony by Ginuwine. Beat chop, swing, and dip, beat chop, swing, and dip. Yep, you all know it, thanks Channing Tatum for putting that awesome image in our heads from Magic Mike as I moved around the room like I was dancing next to him. Sliding the onions into the pan I started swirling my hips to the beat. Now it was my chance for a little dance break, hands-free while I was waiting for the mincemeat to defrost in the microwave. I shimmied over to the boom and then twirled my new dancing partner around. And yep, those hip grinding moves got deeper and sexier. I was in my element just dancing free and was totally in my happy place. Am I painting a good picture for you now?

Back to my spag-bol, add the pasta sauce, simmer, and shimmy. Then the moment really hit me!! Shit!! I need to dance again. This was my 'WHY' I needed to start this business. If not for my own benefit and sanity, but to also share with other women who need the freedom to move. Quick backstory: I danced since I was 4 years old and used to teach dancing in schools. Right up until I had kids and life got a bit and crazy, so I stopped. Can you relate to this?

I decided then and there that this is what I had been missing in my life. Just to dance crazy and I knew that there must be other mums and sister's out there too who felt the same.

From that moment on, I started to put together an awesome dance playlist of my favourite tunes and this got me so excited. The music got louder and louder as I danced down memory lane with my favourite songs to bust out to.

I just kept on dancing in the kitchen until finally Nath came in to check on dinner and saw me all hot and sweaty and said, "what have you been doing?" I said, "just cooking dinner with some swag! Ha- ha." I explained that dinner would be a little longer, as I was having a bit too much fun! He's face lit up with a big smile and he spun the kids around in the kitchen as he could see that I was really happy.

Later, when Nath and I ate dinner, I explained my idea of starting up a second business (I'll tell you about my first business a bit later so stay tuned). I'd even given it a name, Shake It Mumma! The Sister's Dance Party! He was so happy for me and he knew that I needed to do this.

The timing was perfect as I had just been given a challenge by the wonderful Tracy Tully to be Tenacious! At that moment I knew that creating this dance group was going to be my tenacious move. I had to do it. I had to dance! I was on a mission to teach dance again.

The next day I created a Facebook group and advertised on my local mum's page and within the first hour I had almost 30 people wanting to join my group! I sorted out dance insurance and found a venue that would be suitable for the dance class and bang I was off. From having the original idea in my kitchen to running my first class was about a week and a half. Can you tell I was keen to get going?

One of the main comments I heard a lot was "I'm so excited and have been waiting to find something like this to do - Michelle" So I knew that I was getting some good market validation. I was going to do something about this missing void in lots of women's lives, not just in my own life.

The dance group numbers began to grow so quickly with numbers hitting over 100 and selling out in the first month. Suddenly, I needed to find a bigger venue. My sisterhood dance party had become a movement.

The true power of what I was creating hit me when one of my Shake It Mumma's Vanessa, said that she was going to bring her three friends to my dance class next week instead of going out for dinner!! Wow!! what power I had and I didn't even know it!! To come to my class and really take the time out is awesome but to feel so good after doing my class that she had to tell her friends about it and prioritise my class over her dinner plans was truly humbling. Vanessa also said, "I really appreciate how comfortable you make me feel".

This is so important to me, as we all know how hard it is to get women to do something out of their comfort zone, especially with something like dancing, when you're not a dancer and literally have two left feet.

Imagine two rooms. One is dark but lit with positive excited energy. Disco lights are flashing all the colours of the rainbow. In this room, there is a spotlight on the teacher. All the participants come in all shapes and sizes and are pumped to go.

The other is a well-lit gym studio where you feel the spotlight is on you. There is nervous energy in the room that almost comes across as anxiety. You feel like you're being judged before you have even started moving as everyone in the room looks like they could run a marathon at the drop of a hat. You feel that everyone is watching you and start to question your decision to go to that class.

Which room are you going to feel more comfortable in? Which room will you seriously dance like nobody's watching?

> *Guys, check out this news mums' class - highly recommend. I attended for the first time tonight. I have ZERO dance skills, but it was a great workout in a dark room with disco lights so not intimidating at all. And I've got my cardio session in tonight, win."*
> —***Sarah***

Having a space set up like the disco room was my edge, my '**Ultimate Selling Point (USP)**'. In a business having a USP is vital for your survival. It's a busy market out there and you need to stand out amongst your competitors. In my case, it's a dark disco room playing music that my sisters' want to hear (yep, I ask what tunes they want each week) that was my ultimate selling point. This helps to ensure repeat business; everyone walks away hot and sweaty, having had a great time, in an awesome safe environment and a bonus workout too.

The power of what I am doing is still surprising me as after class it's so great to see all the women just laughing, re-enacting the dance moves together and just chatting about themselves and NOT their kids. This is the essence of sisters giving themselves the time to just be women and connecting with others who have all experienced something truly wonderful.

Since I've started this business *Shake It Mumma!* I've had women who are not mums ask to come along. My first response was that I wanted to keep this just for mums as we truly understand the limited time, we have to do something exclusive for ourselves.

However, I realised that to have all women participating, socialising, and willing to try something new needed to be supported. Women who are not mums still feel the pressure of daily life and need this release.

So, all women are welcome of all ages. I've had women from 25-60 join in and everyone can work at their own pace. I know I have what traditionally would be a broad '**Target Audience**' but have had success with keeping it open to all ages, shapes, and sizes. It's not about how good a dancer you are, it's that you move and have a fun time.

That is how I turned my passion into a business. I highly encourage you to find your true passion and build a business around it. It will mean that you will never work a day in your life. So cliche but totally true!

ACTIVITY #1 | What's Missing In Your Life?

I want to inspire you to pick up where you left off, it might not be dancing but it might be netball, tennis, running, arts, singing, swimming. Whatever it is that you stopped, due to kids or life getting a bit crazy.

I encourage you to start it again. I have never felt more full in my life (except those kid birth moments, they were kind of important!) after doing this for myself again. It's so important to give yourself the time.

So now I've shared my passion with you, I want you to write down here:
I am going to start_____go and do it now! Look and see if activities are offered in your local community. If it isn't, do something about it. Create a Facebook group and see if there is interest out there. That's it, you have now started to create your own business. Good luck!

ACTIVITY #2 | Finding Your Happy Place

What's your Jam? You all know mine is Pony now. Go and put your favourite jam on!! Close your eyes and feel the beat in your soul.

Visualise what dance moves you want to do. Now open your eyes and DO them!! Don't think about it, just do it.

Whenever life is a bit much, remember your happy place. Take a minute to listen to your favourite song and dance it out.

> *So, pump up the music when you can and have a little dance party between home schooling, juggling work, and the million and one other things you have to do! Just don't forget to dance!"*
> — **Tiffany Droge**

Now from my love of dance to my love of product design and giving parents freedom on their family adventures, read about where my entrepreneurial mindset all started.

My Innovative Moments

How being a mum gave me the opportunity to innovate and solve real parenting problems.

A bit more about my road to becoming an entrepreneur. *Shake It Mumma* was not my first business. Let me share with you how my entrepreneurial journey started.

I felt trapped when I became a parent as the baby industry didn't provide products that suited my active lifestyle. I'm a Health and Physical Education teacher and a lover of the outdoors. I wanted to create a business around fun, freedom, and adventures for parents. So, they felt that they could easily get out on their adventure with their little ones.

After all, the adventure shouldn't stop when you have kids. Being a Mum meant that I was now a consumer in the baby industry, I joined the dots and thought why not start up a business around this? It ticked a lot of boxes. As you know baby season is open season, it's all year round! I knew that this journey was going to be a huge part of my life, so why not join business with pleasure? The result was …

Jumply, "Adventure Gear for Family Fun".

Jumply is on a mission to create the best gear for adventurous families, based on real mum innovation that solves everyday parenting problems. I did not want parents' adventures to be dictated by pram limitations or the feeling of overwhelm just to leave the house.

Is this you too? Dreading leaving the house even for a simple outing? This was me, so I decided to do something about it.

Jumply creates a world where you can walk out of the house with just ONE bag allowing for an effortless escape! This makes it easy for parents like you to experience the true freedom you deserve, while giving you the valour to tackle any family adventure. *Jumply* offers a unique product range that is great value, while providing personalised service you can trust.

> *How awesome it was to head off the beaten track on our first adventure with our adventure carrier. So lightweight and easy to use, I carried my 8-month-old for a 2 hour walk with ease. He looked so relaxed and even had a little nap during that time.*
>
> *With so many pockets this backpack is so much more than a carrier it's also the ultimate nappy bag. Thanks, Jumply for not only an awesome product but great service. We can't wait to get lots more use out of our purchase and not feel the need to have to lug along a pram.*
>
> *We have been telling everyone who wants to listen about this product because we just want to share our excitement!"*
> —***Aussie Mum, Jo***

My first product that really launched my brand was the *Adventure Nappy Backpack*. It was a baby bag on the inside and an adventure bag on the outside. I combined specialised nappy storage with rugged "go-anywhere" features. Its unisex design meant it was great for mums as well as dads and perfect for Australian families. With its water-repellent outer shell and 17 cleverly placed pockets and sections, it truly was a unique Nappy Backpack.

I was sick of carrying an oversized shoulder bag around that just didn't suit my active lifestyle. It was also killing my back and shoulder from its non-ergonomic design. Have you also experienced this aching pain? We as mums seriously put our bodies through enough than needing to also cop the ache from a nappy bag that's meant to make our lives easier. Am I speaking to you yet? This was my chance to design something new and fresh.

The idea came to me in the early hours of the morning as I was breastfeeding my daughter Tanner. I was massaging my sore neck from dragging my incredibly heavy nappy bag around all day. Suddenly, I had the urge to sketch the design for a new nappy backpack. I remember being so hyped up from developing my new idea, I couldn't get back to sleep. I knew I was onto something. This was the moment that would start the next chapter of my life.

A few months later, my prototypes were ready. I couldn't believe it. I had my first 4 samples ready to 'road test'. We took it to the snow, beach, adventure walking trails, and the zoo until we had the perfect product.

The *Adventure Nappy Backpack* was successfully funded on Kickstarter in 2018. This Kickstarter Campaign was perhaps one of the most stressful things that Nath and I have ever done in partnership. Keep in mind, we have travelled around the world and experienced our fair share of adventures and stressful situations.

I want to share a story with you that illustrates the persistence and strength that I have as not only a business woman but as a fighter in life. I have been brought up lucky enough to experience the magic of the snow. I skied since I was four years old and knew that traveling to different snowfields around the world was going to be a big part of my life. Nath and I worked in South Lake Tahoe in America, Big White in Canada, and then in Hakuba in Japan, truly living it up as you do in your early 20's. This is where there is a turn in my story and I was reminded of the cold hard danger that Mother Nature can throw at you at any second, no matter how experienced you are in the snow.

I had been working in Japan for a few months and had just experienced a massive snowfall over the last 48 hours!! So, like any avid snow adventurer, I needed to get out there. Things were going well and I was cruising down the mountain on my snowboard with Nath and my friends. I particularly love going up on the side of the run as that is where there is always more snow-swept by other skiers, meaning deeper snow for me. As I was snowboarding to the edge of the run, I lost control and tumbled over the side gathering more and more speed as I fell. Goggles filled with snow and I could not see. I was buried, Mother Nature had swallowed me whole!

Nath had no idea where I was and he was only about 20 metres downhill from me, but I was nowhere to be seen. This was so terrifying. I didn't know which way was up. I was panicking and inhaling the fine snowflakes. I was also wearing a brace to support my lower back which meant that my movement was restricted, so I couldn't get to my feet to unclip my bindings to move free. From what I could feel my head was downhill and my feet above me. It was all white!

Somehow a moment of calm came over me and I knew I needed to fight to get out. No one was there to help me, so I had to do this on my own. I pulled my jacket up over my mouth and created a seal to take a big breath in without snowflakes filling my lungs. This gave me the power to punch through the snow bursting out like a whale coming up for air and jumping out of the water in spectacular form. However, minus the spectacular form for me. I started thrashing the snow to compact it and try to make a firm base for me to get out of. I was smacking the snow so hard that it was working.

I managed to form a ledge that was strong enough to support my body to wiggle out of like a fat seal, as my feet were still attached to my snowboard. It was like I had a tail and wiggling was all I could do. I then commando crawled back onto the run, as skiers were whizzing by. They had no idea that I could have almost died no more than 20 meters away from them. I rode down to Nath and my friends, and they could instantly see that something was wrong. I told them what had happened, and Nath felt so guilty that he was not there to help me. From that moment I knew that I was never going to give up and would always fight to get out of a tight place. No matter if in business or in my personal life. I was a fighter and determined to make a difference in this life.

Back to the main story of my entrepreneurial journey to fight to get to where I want to go. This brings us to funding our *Adventure Nappy Backpack*.

Having been in business together for a number of years, as well as raising little humans had its stressful moments. However, Kickstarter tested our marriage!

Between the multiple failed video shoots (where 'someone' forgot to press record on the drone), the million script rewrites, and a screaming toddler who would not cooperate, I didn't know if we could ever get through it. However, once the campaign got going and was successful things started to calm down. I realised my design for the *Adventure Nappy Backpack* was about to be made and I felt so proud of my efforts.

The innovation didn't stop there; the *Adventure Nappy Backpack* was just the tip of my innovative iceberg. I went on to redesign changing wallets, pram organisers, picnic mats and now have the *Adventure Carrier*. Combining a baby and toddler carrier and a nappy backpack. Its unique storage allows you to only take one bag, giving you freedom on your next family adventure. It can hold up to a 15kg baby and they can go in there from 6 to 7 months old.

Have you felt the weight of needing to take so many bags as well as a pram on your family adventures? Sometimes the overwhelm can feel so exhausting that you don't have the strength to leave the house once you're all packed to go. Have you ever wished that there was ONE bag that would do it all, as well as carry your baby or toddler? Well, my friend, I'm here to throw you a lifeline and it's the **Adventure Carrier**.

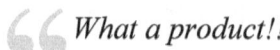

What a product!!

Hands down what an increditble design!

I am a Mum to a 4-year-old and a 1-year-old, so I am constantly busy and always on the go. We recently did a camping trip over Easter and this carrier is by far the best one I have ever come across! I was able to carry my 1yr old around while setting up and packing down the tent / camping equipment with pure ease.

The carrier is so comfy and padded around my back, the pockets on the side are convenient and so easy to access while wearing the carrier.

The front pockets hold so much stuff (my kids come with a lot) and the space underneath where my 1 yr old is positioned, is useful to stuff those excess jumpers under. The sunshade is amazing for keeping him out of the sun and the water proof cover does its job 110%.

There is nothing about this carrier that I could fault, every family should own one of these. It's practical, comfortable to wear and my 1yr old LOVES IT! Great job on an amazing product."
—New Zealand Mum, Kate Southgate

The idea for the *Adventure Carrier* came to me after we went to the travel expo and were using our *Adventure Nappy Backpack* and a framed carrier separately. The carrier we had was only a frame and seat with no back support, so was not very comfortable to wear and had no pockets. I borrowed it from my parents. They used to put me in it back in the '80s. I'm sure your parents may still have one kicking around too.

Nath had taken a photo of me carrying the *Adventure Nappy Backpack*, holding both kids' hands and carrying the framed carrier for no real reason. Yes, perhaps he could have offered to carry something is what I'm sure you're all thinking.

Quick story about Nath and I. The first time that I spoke to him was at the beach with some friends. I actually swallowed a fly and was trying to not act like I had just swallowed a fly, as I was instantly attracted to him. This was not a good look for me. I don't even think that he noticed at first, so it meant that I was doing a good job covering it up. He asked if I was ok, and I couldn't even tell him what was happening. I then managed to get the fly up in the most lady-like way I could (not very lady-like at all) and we had a big laugh about it. He still asked for my number from my friend, so I must not have been too off-putting. Perhaps this was a moment that changed him, and he saw the really funny side of me that he might not have seen if I was trying to act 'cool' in front of him. We ran and laughed on the beach like we were Danny and Sandy in the movie *Grease* and the rest is history.

Back to my story of how I came up with the idea for the *Adventure Carrier*. I was looking back at the photos from our day's adventure, that was when it hit me of combining the two. This was my next moment of greatness.

I innovated a nappy backpack combined with a baby carrier that would be carry-on size making it the perfect travel gear for airplanes, going to the zoo, aquarium, walking tracks, markets, expos, and shows. This would have a bit more of an urban feel than those big baby hiking carriers. After all, I was designing it with mums in mind, so it needed to be lightweight and compact.

The *Adventure Carrier* was going to solve so many problems of not needing to take a pram, a separate nappy backpack, and carrier. It would also keep the little one safe in busy areas, supporting babies and toddlers with special needs that have limited mobility, and keeping your little one safe and away from germs.

> *Was amazed how much could be packed in the back. Little fella loved his new transportation. I felt no strain on my body. It's super easy to take on and off. We even managed to test drive it at shows where there are crowds, I still felt very mobile. People asked where did I get this from, I just pointed to the logo which was all they need to know."*
> **—Aussie Dad, Hristijan**

Wow, all the amazing things that this *Adventure Carrier* can do! However, there is a huge hidden benefit that might not be obvious, and this is the increase in mental health. The Adventure Carrier gives you more flexibility and freedom to experience the outdoors. Meaning, spending time outdoors especially in green spaces reduces your symptoms of anxiety, depression and improves mood and self-esteem. Did you know that spending just 20 minutes a day outside in nature is enough for you to reap the rewards of positive mental health? You can read more about it from my blog "The Benefits of Being Outside and Links to Positive Mental Health" (*see link at the end of the chapter*).

When I first saw the design for this carrier backpack it looked just like a normal backpack. I said to the manufacturer I was after a carrier backpack. When she opened it and revealed the 5-point safety harness inside I was blown away by the compact structure. It was a very basic design, but I knew that I could make it 100 times better with my mummy innovative touches. I added as many extra pockets and storage solutions as I could and jacked up the ergonomic design to ensure that it was super comfortable for my parents who were wearing it. This design process took about 12 months and three prototypes later, as well as thousands of dollars spent on testing it to ensure it complied with the correct safety standards.

Quick story...

One day I took my kids to the aquarium on the train on my own as Nath was doing something with the boys' AKA drinking. I used my new *Adventure Carrier* for Chase while Tanner walked next to me, as she is five, she doesn't need the pram. I think it's important to get kids to walk and not miss any opportunity to exercise. I guess this is the Physical Education teacher in me coming out!

I felt like a rockstar walking up and down the stairs with a true sense of valour like I had won the battle against "The Pram". It felt effortless at the train station and not needing to wait for the lift at the aquarium. I was experiencing the true freedom that the *Adventure Carrier* had to offer.

The number of parents at the aquarium who were pushing around empty prams or holding up their kids to see the exhibits was crazy, as well as carrying a nappy bag. I know we have all been there at some stage. However, the *Adventure Carrier* is the solution to living a life that allows you to just take one bag on your next family adventure and you guessed it, no pram needed! If this sounds good to you, you're in the right place.

I hopped on the tram heading home and saw a family trying to hoist their pram up onto the tram, but they couldn't. The kids were very similar in age (2.5 and 5) to mine, and I thought to myself you need my *Adventure Carrier*! They ended up bailing on the tram ride, this really validated the need for this product.

Back to it...

I knew that the idea was good but once again funding was an issue. We took to Kickstarter in 2020 once more to get our *Adventure Carrier* funded. We needed it to be funded as the production had already started.

I wouldn't recommend doing it this way, as it did put a lot of financial stress on us. Sadly, our campaign was not successful. AHHHH!! We were screwed.

We miscalculated our Kickstarter goal of $10k and perhaps this product was not right for the platform. Setting the financial goal is a strategy in itself. If you set your goal too high, you may not reach it and get nothing. If you set it too low and reach it the funds might not be enough to cover production costs. So, it's a game. We lost, big time.

In our reflections, we believe that the production time and specific weight range the product catered to might have been against us. For example, the product was not going to arrive for at least 3 months and in that time the baby's weight might not fit the 15kg weight requirements.

A quick bit of information about Kickstarter.com. It's a platform to help businesses fund ideas and projects just like ours. If you want a project to put into production, you need to pledge for it. The business will set a target goal, ours was $10k. If you reach that goal in your campaign period (ours was 28 days) you get the funds. However, if you don't, you get nothing. It is a risk-free way to shop as a consumer, if the project or idea doesn't get funded you don't pay any money.

You have to make your campaign stand out and it's all about having a flashy video that demonstrates your product and catches your audience in the first few seconds (6 seconds to be exact). We spent over $2k on a professional video, you don't need to do this, but we said if we ever did another Kickstarter, we would get a professional videographer to do it. The first time we used Kickstarter we did it ourselves, as you read above it was extremely difficult and almost ended in divorce.

It was very frustrating that the investment of our professional video did not pay off but at least we have some great content that we can continue to use. There is lots of information out there about how to run Kickstarter campaigns and don't get me wrong it was a lot of fun but is also a game that may or may not pay off. Just prepare yourself for all possible outcomes.

The year 2020 was not kind to us as a lot of businesses found and being an outdoor family adventure brand really did take a hit, as we didn't have any savings. We were sure that Kickstarter would be successful so we didn't have a Plan B. This was silly and not good business, don't ever do this.

Our bank loans were all tapped out, there was only one more source of finance that we could access. That was another parent loan. We needed to go there again (we're still paying off our previous one and do thank our parents for their continual support). Luckily, we were able to obtain this loan and, in the process, presented a formal five-year business plan, including a budget.

We were very lucky that we had this support and were able to complete the first run for our *Adventure Carrier*. We are now faced with the challenge of getting it out there. Which is harder than you think. There is no such thing as overnight success. Quite often you never hear about the years of hard work that go into a business and how they get their big break.

This year is all about scaling up for us, we know that we have amazing products that solve real parent problems, and we have a very specific target audience. Now we have to focus on our marketing to get our product's out into the world. That's easier said than done.

Marketing is super complex. We had put our trust into two different agencies over the 5 years and had seen minimal results, none that would reflect at least a $15k marketing spend. We couldn't afford to keep paying them for no sales. I understand that it does take time to build up the data required to run a successful marketing campaign. However, when you are as boot strapped as we were, we couldn't afford to not be getting any returns. Especially after being with the companies for around 4 to 5 months.

Our solution was Nath upskilling himself to learn as best as he could about Facebook Ads, Google Ads, Email Marketing, and Drop shipping up until we could look at another marketing agency to run our advertising for us. By upskilling, he would also have more of an understanding of what questions to ask the agency and what to look for in greater detail. That's if we go back there again. So, if you have the time and are willing to learn, surround yourself with people who will teach you.

It sometimes seems that our roadblocks are endless. When you think you have a new lead, it turns out to be a dead end. When you think you're eligible for Research and Development Grant funding and jump through multiple hoops. Only to be given the wrong advice and your business is too small to even apply. Even after changing over your business entity to be eligible. Boom!! Another roadblock. Giving up is not an option!

Roadblocks will happen in your business but it's all about how strong your WHY is, that's what will keep you going.

> *Remember if it was meant to be easy, then everybody would do it.   You have to fight for what you want!"*
> *—Tiffany Droge, adapted from Tom Hanks in A League of Their Own*

ABOUT THE AUTHOR

TIFFANY DROGE

Something that continues to give me strength through these roadblocks is asking myself the question 'what now?' So, this happened, and it sucks but…… what now? Asking yourself this question automatically helps you think about your next move and not dwell on things you can't control. Although it is important to reflect. You need to get on with the job. After all, changing people's lives is no easy feat but I know that you can do anything you put your mind to. If I can do it, so can you. I know our big break is just around the corner.

Starting a business is very rewarding and it's a legacy for our children. However, you need to be able to answer these four starting questions in detail before you decide to build a new business:

1. **WHY** do you want to start a business?

2. **WHAT** problem are you solving?

3. **WHO** is your target audience?

4. **WHAT** is your Ultimate Selling Point (USP) that will make you stand out among your competitors?

> *It might take you a few goes at finding your dream business but the more you do it, the better you get at it, like anything in life"*
> — ***Tiffany Droge***

If my story has resonated with you and you love the idea of an effortless escape while giving you the freedom to conquer the world with true valour. Then make sure you check out the Adventure Carrier at jumply.com.au now.

Thank you for reading about my story. I hope that you have enjoyed it, and it has inspired you to fight for what you want.

Tiffany's Ten Top Tips for Success

1. Find your support crew, can be other people in non- competing business.

2. Find a mentor.

3. Network in a genuine way at every opportunity.

4. Conduct detailed market research.

5. Use Canva.com to create your content.

6. Use Trello.com as an information capturing system.

7. Invest time in yourself in marketing courses, until you can outsource.

8. Outsource the first thing that does not bring you joy.

9. Evaluate after every product launch/campaign.

10. These notes will help you improve for the future.

Connect with Tiffany, Founder of *Shake It Mumma* at:

Website: www.shakeitmumma.com.au/

Facebook: www.facebook.com/groups/shakeitmumma

Jumply:

For all inquiries or retail and wholesale opportunities please email tiffany@jumply.com.au

facebook.com/jumply.au

instagram.com/jumply.au

5

BECOMING THE ALIGNED LEADER
THE ANSWER: LEADERSHIP FATIGUE SYNDROME

by SAM DEAN

JUNE 2014. I was at my farewell party. We were at a beautiful golf club. It was cold but the fire heaters created warmth. The atmosphere was one of celebration. The business I was leaving was a large accounting firm, there were over 100 people celebrating the end of the financial year and the ridiculous amount of work we'd done up to the end of it. The secondary celebration was farewelling myself and another partner who was retiring after decades in the business. Here is my first rule break – I wasn't retiring I resigned. The first partner to do so in the 75-year history of the business.

I was wearing my hair short and dark something to this day I go "why?" My clothes were dark and drab with a hint of red, my one attempt to throw some power and colour into my space. My demeanour was heavy, not just in the extra weight I was carrying, but in my posture and the expression on my face. It was a posture of protection and curtailing. I was a woman who looked like the world was on my shoulders and all I wanted was to curl up, sit in a corner and not carry it anymore.

On paper and by societal measures, I was successful.

I had been making great money and truth be told even if myself and my fellow colleagues didn't hit our financial targets for the quarter, we still got paid. I had the prestige of calling myself a partner in a long standing large regional firm. A level I had always aspired to and considered the pinnacle for any professional career.

I was a leader of a business turning over eight figures annually. Even today that's a rare thing for a woman to do. Although, at the time I wasn't aware just how rare.

I was a nationally recognised speaker and thought leader on how to introduce advisory services into accounting practices.

I wasn't physically sick by cultural norms. No big trauma, no viably "acceptable reasons". Ignoring the fact, I was depressed, unfit, overweight, burnt out and an alcoholic.

These are normal symptoms that many professional business leaders experience. I could see everyone around me looked to be in a similar predicament and, "work hard, party hard" was the call.

So why was I leaving?

In fact, the logical pragmatic side of me wasn't even sure why. My training and upbringing were screaming – "what are you doing?" filling me with doubts and fears. The inner script was playing "it will be ok, just keep going".

BUT I KNEW – a voice had told me seven weeks earlier "get out or you will die". This is not where you need to be. I was walking away from a successful accounting business that gave me financial security and "success", to save my life. Not that this was the reason I gave anyone at the time.

What was I actually leaving?

The business that I was leaving was a good business, but it was no longer safe for me and my vision.

The business was run on rules written over centuries ago. Change was fine if it didn't cost time, money or God forbid, discomfort. Emotions and feelings were only allowed if they were "good" and not "too much". Safe conversation was having them when the person involved was not in the room.

Values were something we hung on the wall – because the marketing people said we needed to have them. Vision and purpose were to make budget. If something of value couldn't be measured by a spreadsheet, it didn't count.

Business decisions were made from comfort and on how it has always been done. They were based on transactions rather than relationships. People and the energy and skills they bring, were measured on spreadsheets, valued on how much time they could bill.

If you put it on a spreadsheet, things will happen.

Your engagement in the business is how much you are seen. First one in, last one out. Working weekends is a hero's cry.

Time was meant to be charged. The busier you are the more money you make.

Don't bring your problems to work. Work to live. What a load of crap. It was a place where I, like so many others were:

- Unseen
- Unheard
- Burnt-out.

Do you know what? This was all unintentional, everyone was doing the best they could with the rules and tools they had.

One thing I know for sure, is that I was not where or who I was supposed to be. I was where I thought I *should be*. They *should* be set by the patriarch system that has been built over generations way before I came along. Yet it was the framework I used to get me this place.

I would like to say (as I believed at the time) that all I needed to do was walk away and do things for myself and escape the stressors. I was at the top of my game. I knew what it took to run a successful business. I had the credentials, the programs and business runs on the board to prove it. I had been doing the leadership courses, marketing workshops and learning whatever skills I could, particularly those soft skills like emotional intelligence.

I could do this. Move on. I didn't need that place; I could build my own business with the framework I had from scratch without the legacy issues and different people.

But as it turned out…that didn't happen!

Despite the different business model and people who did make me feel seen and heard I was still running with the old rules, the old patterns based on the *should* rules that just do not work anymore. I had to break and re-write them for myself. At this point I had no awareness, knowledge, or tools on how to do this. I was empty handed and suffering from leadership fatigue.

Every coping mechanism I had learnt or been given to help me survive, was just getting in the way of my success. My rules were being exposed for what they really were. A matrix. Glass walls stacking one behind another. I thought I was at rock bottom in 2014 when I left the big firm, but it was only rock middle. More was to come.

It took me a while to sort this but fortunately my inner wisdom is persistent! While the big shout or tap in May 2014 was heard after many warnings, the issue was not just the place I was in but the fact that I was completely out of alignment. Every time I headed in a direction that *should* have been right, the same patterns and issues kept arising.

NO ONE had ever told me that happiness and success is an internal play and that any external success is directly linked to the amount of work you do on YOU and understanding your rules and play book, the psychology of yourself.

To quote Tony Robbins *"**Success in life is 80% psychology and 20% mechanics.**"* I struggled with this ratio for a while but it wasn't until I started to work on the psychology of ME most of the time, did my success and happiness start to flow.

Today it's been over seven years. I'm writing from my desk overlooking my acreage property, admiring the view of the dam outside and listening to the Australian native birds make their way through the day.

I'm getting ready to ride my horse, Larry. You see, I had been dreaming of spending more time with my horses and now over the years I have realised what an important aspect of my mental and physical health riding them is. Having the time and space to ride and compete with them, just wouldn't fit the old rules and model of business that I was in, that earned me the money I needed, to actually ride Larry regularly.

It wasn't long before I competed my dressage horse at the Queensland State Championship during the week. Would you believe during that period my business sales increased and I competed without the guilt, or the previous mind chatter I had of "you should be working".

In fact, the number of times I ride my horse during the week is a KPI we measure in our business as myself and my team knows it's a key driver to the business's success. Counter intuitive you may think, but I'll explain later!

More importantly I like to measure how I'm feeling as a KPI. Gone is the heaviness both in physical weight and the weight of the world. I no longer have to carry excess weight in order to protect myself from external forces.

One of my closet friends who worked with the old me (pre- 2014 me) described it this way

 It's as if a semitransparent cloak has slowly been coming off, revealing your vibrancy and passion that was always there but now able to shine."
— **Sam Dean**

I now own BlueprintHQ, a business I foundered based on the Toni Morrison quote "If there's a book that you want to read but it hasn't been written, you must write it." Well BlueprintHQ is my version of that. We develop programs and services that I needed, so other expert leaders can develop businesses on their own terms.

It is also the working business model of what we are trying to achieve for others. It's a very different business, I have an amazing business partner as well as collaborative and inspiring people around me. We are building a business on our own terms that is both challenging and uncomfortable at times. We are making mistakes and celebrating them along with our successes. We have boundaries and rules written and agreed upon. We have worked hard, had tough conversations and if we get stuff wrong, we've owned it and fixed it. I've made difficult changes in my life.

Hard work is learning to love yourself, questioning the stories we've been given and written for yourself. Breaking the societal norms that hold you or you hold on to. Breaking up with people that drag your emotional energy and wellbeing down.

Is every day a joy? No. I still have my bad days where crawling under the covers feels like the only viable option. I just don't fight this feeling anymore. I lean in.

Success is measured on a variety of metrics. Yes, making money and having a successful business is still one of them, but I've learnt that success and the metrics that drive it are not what society tells you they are but what YOU WANT THEM TO BE, based on your own terms.

To come to those terms in the current furious storm of overwhelm, over consumption and distraction is a challenge. However, that's what is needed. Until you do this, any success that you are aiming for is limited. Particularly when that success is based on definitions that aren't yours.

How do we do this?

Firstly, as with my story let's define what the actual problem is before we try to solve it? As Albert Einstein said:

> *If I had an hour to solve a problem, I'd spend 55 minutes thinking about the problem and 5 minutes thinking about the solution!"*
> **—Albert Einstein**

This is where I think we lose a lot of energy, we are constantly adopting solutions and not truly understanding the problem we are trying to solve.

Here's the problem – how, when we are exhausted and suffer from Leadership Fatigue Syndrome, do we do anything about it when any attempt to solve the fatigue just adds to it?

Let's start with defining it.

Leadership Fatigue Syndrome is the result of leaders being out of alignment with where they want to be. It's caused by not having the skills to figure out what that is. Then there's the skills to keep them from veering off that alignment with their desires, especially when they experience the highs and lows that life throws at them.

It has been around for a long time and growing at an overwhelming pace. I've suffered it myself and I see it in the eyes of our clients and the leaders I talk to every day. Most discussions around the causes are based on societal and external pressures. There is too much work, information, consumption, decisions to be made. While I agree that these are all contributing factors, these can't be controlled externally, only how we deal with them.

It's not something that can be fixed with a holiday, time off or better sleep. These certainly help you feel rested but it's not a physical fatigue. Do you ever go on holiday, come back feeling rested and then four weeks later, are just as fatigued as you were before you left, if not more? This is a symptom of **Leadership Fatigue Syndrome (LFS)**.

How about more personal development, leadership training and tools like breathing apps for coping? Like most others, this is where I started. These help to some degree but if this was all that was required, Leadership Fatigue Syndrome wouldn't be the epidemic it is now.

Have you ever looked at a painting on the wall and it's driven you crazy because it was slightly out of alignment, and you couldn't fix it because you had no control over it? This is what I'm talking about. This is the nagging feeling that says something's not quite right or I'm fatigued and why can't I do everything that I need to do? This work is addressing that problem.

You see the problem needs an internal fix. We have to look at our skills and start questioning the rules we are running to break the *LFS* cycle. As leaders, we need to bring ourselves into alignment with our true selves.

What Are the Steps That You Can Take If You Find Yourself Suffering From Leadership Fatigue?

I'm guessing the thoughts are popping up with "I'm just too overwhelmed", "I don't have enough time", "I know I'm in a shit storm, but I still need to earn money" and versions of the above. I'm with you on these and they are all valid, but there is hope. Start simple and with the intention of being consistent over time with small steps. Our fatigue was built over decades therefore, it needs to be addressed slowly and consistently to unwind it.

There are a few things you need to know before we start.

Firstly, this is about increasing our internal skills and using them to align ourselves. What's super interesting is that as leaders, we're not equipped for this. Think about the last time you sat down and asked yourself what you wanted and what you desired?

This may seem counterintuitive but great leaders need to be upfront and leading by design. If you lead people in business and/or within your family or communities, and you want them to be safe and meeting their goals while working all together, you need to be aligned yourself. Otherwise, they're also going to be out of alignment.

This is not taught in traditional leadership programs whereby the basis for most is teaching leaders to lead or manage other people, not themselves. These are still important skills but only after you understand which ones contribute to your alignment.

Secondly, this is about you.

We often blame the situation, the patriarch system, COVID-19, or people around us for our own personal shit shows. At the end of the day, they are ours and are mostly internal. Fortunately, that means you are the only one that can fix YOU and YOU hold the power.

There is no doubt that external forces have helped get you to where you are. What I learnt was that until I gave up trying to change the people around me and stop bitching about them, the change and growth I worked for, was fleeting at best.

You also have to stop being so hard on yourself. Now this isn't easy. When I started listening to myself, I noticed I was my own worst critic. The negative thoughts like "I don't deserve this success", were coming from me, not others. Becoming aware of this is crucial to staying in alignment.

*What does it look like to call yourself an **Aligned Leader**?*

- Clarity on what you desire, who you want to be and a plan to get there. You are clear on what success looks like to you.
- Know what keeps you aligned.
- What daily habits you keep.
- Who gets to be around them?
- The rules they live by.
- Amazing boundaries – that protect them and the skills to make them happen.

A great way to think of the alignment is like a plumb line in surveying. A plumb line is used to determine a vertical line directly to the centre of gravity of the earth. They ensure everything is aligned, centred and right.

There are three elements that make up this simple tool:

- The centre of gravity of the earth,
- the plumb line – which includes the plumb string, and
- the plumb bob.

In relation to the Aligned Leader:

- The centre of gravity of the earth – leaders' desires.
- Plumb string – the plan to get to those desires.
- Plumb bob – the behaviours, skills, people, and boundaries that keep you in alignment.

Centre Of Gravity - Work Out What You Desire and Your Definition Of Success.

The biggest thing that helped me combat my leadership fatigue, was getting clarity on what I wanted and what success looked like for me. Honestly, it probably started off originally knowing what I didn't want.

Without this process you'll always be a little bit off and defaulting back to paths and habits that you want to leave behind.

Up until now, most of what we think we want is based on what we think we *should* want. The amount of subconscious societal pressures that we're under can be overwhelming. Add to this, the patriarch system where this pressure stems from. Success is often being defined simply as more staff, more offices, more money etc.

Let's cut through the *should* noise. When thinking of what you want, ask yourself these questions:

- How do I want to be feeling?
- Who do I want to hang out with?
- How do I want to be treated?
- Who do I want to be?
- What do my days look like?
- What type of work will I be doing?

Here are some tips:

- Ask the question and write down anything that comes to mind.
- Be specific. Just saying I want to feel free, is too broad. Instead try: "I will be feeling free because I have built a financial fortress for my family, and I am earning enough to meet my desired lifestyle."
- Forget all the reasons why it can't be done, think only in terms of what you want.

Connect with how it makes you feel and what it would look like. You need to be able to hold that feeling and vision to stay aligned even when things go sour. This is your centre of gravity.

Plumb string – the plan to get there.

You need a starting point and some steps outlined in the continuum to get from where you are to where you want to be. Note that what you want and how you get there is dynamic and will continue to evolve. It will need constant revising. Now have look and ask:

What's the most important thing I can work on in the short-term that will give me more comfort and energy, even if it's just a little bit more right now?

What's the most important thing to start working on first? What can I do that fits into what I'm already doing with the resources I have?

Plumb bob - to keep your string aligned.

We build the weight of this over time, and the following contributes to the plumb bob with:

- Internal skills
- Rules we play by
- Who we play with
- Boundaries we set and keep.

These all contribute to the weight that keeps us in alignment and energised.

INTERNAL SKILLS

Here are a couple to get you started and have become my superpowers!

Creating space in your day when there is no time.

You can't create time, but you can create space in your day. Think in terms of: What's the most important thing I'm going to work on today?

There's really a lot of things that we're doing as leaders that we need to just stop doing. So, that's where this question comes in. And if you can really clarify that, then that gives you a framework you can work with to make easy decisions throughout the day when people and life get in the way. Build the confidence to say, "No! that's not on my agenda today!"

This helps if you often get to the end of the day and think "what did I actually do?" I'm exhausted but I didn't finish what I wanted to get done.

Discover What Grounds YOU And Provides Your Energy.

And no, coffee is not the answer.

One of the tricks to staying in alignment is being grounded. It works the same as a rugby player getting ready for a tackle. They set themselves and draw the strength into the bottom half of their body, decreasing the chance of being knocked over. Finding your way to do this with your day or resetting it during the day, starts building your alignment plumb bob.

So how do you start this process, is there something that grounds you when you do it regularly? Something that if you don't do, you turn into a grouch/raving lunatic/sloth? For me, it's riding my horses in the morning, and I reset during the day by taking time to go outside and soak in sun.

RULES WE PLAY BY

Rules are interesting and they weren't something I cottoned on to early. There are two aspects to rules when building your plumb bob. Becoming aware of the ones you blindingly follow, questioning them and re-writing rules of your own that help keep you maintain alignment.

We have been convinced as humans that if you play by the rules, then you will be successful.

Too often, those rules were created in the last centuries by men and for men. At times they are not relevant to our modern world of today.

Here are three examples:

1. **Success measures commonly used should be accepted**

I can write a whole book of examples but here's one for you – the Body Mass Index (BMI). Often thought of as a success measure for heath and ideal body weight.

The BMI was written by a scholar (not a doctor) over 200 years ago to measure population for statistical purposes, not individual health. It doesn't take into account the variances of at least half the population - women and non-Caucasian males.

The next time you find you are judging yourself or making a decision based on an arbitrary accepted measure such as the BMI, research it and decide for yourself if it's a measure worthwhile using.

2. **Your personal and business life should be kept separate**

Uh no, you can't split yourself. The emotions you feel between 9-5, the energy you deplete – the toxicity you expose yourself to - does not magically disappear when you walk out the office door or turn your laptop off!

The extension to this is to leave your problems at work or at home. As a leader I shockingly bought into this one and didn't dispute it.

Our workplaces and businesses are where we spend a good chunk of our time, and for a lot of people, it's their most consistent community. Somehow, we think it's ok to spend time and not feel comfortable sharing all of ourselves, the good and the bad, with people who don't want to know or take the time to get to know us, under the disguise of "professionalism". You're here to do the job.

Often, when we switch our emotions on and off, this can manifest itself in all sorts of disruptive ways. For example, leading to illnesses and unhealthy relationships.

Any definition of success must encompass all aspects of YOU to attempt to be aligned.

3. **Working hard means time in the seat – grinding the hours. The more you work the more success you have.**

The thing is that hard work is not working more hours or being the busiest person. Nor are the number of hours you work a direct correlation to the precise amount of success you will encounter. This only distracts you from the real work of becoming aligned.

WHO WE PLAY WITH?

I can categorically tell you that breaking up with people that drag you down emotionally whether intentionally or not, is one of your biggest plays in overcoming LFS.

In my need to be liked by others, this was my weakest link in building my plumb bob weight. And until recently a recurring pattern of mine.

You can tell who these people are by the time you spend talking about them, trying to correct them, get them to do things they said they could. Sometimes you might use the term – "their intentions are good" or "they are nice but…".

These are not the people who challenge you and push you to be better. When I say *people who challenge you*, they are a crucial element of your team, but only if you respect them. Don't let people challenge or judge you if you wouldn't let them on your horse!

BOUNDARIES WE SET AND KEEP

This really takes the time to build skill around.

Boundaries work like your house boundary line – they should be clear, communicated and when broken, there are consequences.

When someone needs to cross your house boundary line, they ask permission to do so and you either let them in or not. If they break this, you call the police.

What are your boundaries? Your house, you call the police there. Again, start small.

To everyone reading this, it's time to start questioning why you are exhausted and to put yourself first. Understand that the problem is our internal alignment as leaders and that this can be solved.

Solving it is not easy but necessary if you want to experience different results from what you are getting now. The surprising part for me is how much more fun I'm having now and I'm only just getting started!

I encourage you to start questioning what you are aligning yourself to. Find your centre of gravity – it is different from everyone else and yours will be unique. Then build your plumb line.

I am so passionate about helping leaders align and break the LFS cycle and work on how good IT can get for them, that we have developed a program that does just that.

At **BlueprintHQ** our main game is helping dynamic business leaders to create a habitat of safety, accountability and growth for their business and its people on their own terms. We know that before we can help any leader do this, they must be aligned.

Without this alignment they are just too damn tired.

I am so aware of this issue and have walked in these shoes myself. Until I started aligning myself nothing seemed quite right, and I wasn't achieving the success I wanted. I have created the program that I needed, **The Aligned Leader**, a six-week program that offers you the safety and process to explore and question what you've always done and create a plan to build and maintain your alignment over time. If this interests you, I'd love you to jump online and go to our *Apply to Work with Us* page (www.blueprinthq.com.au/apply), have a quick look at the video and fill in the application. From there, we can start having a conversation to see if we're a great match.

In the meantime, please take some time and space to look after yourself. It doesn't need to be a whole day. Just start small - five or ten minutes each day, do some kind of self-care. The biggest return on investment I ever received from any of the education and coaching time I spent was the time I worked on myself. I'm certain you will find the same thing for you too.

Sam's Ten Top Tips

1. **Align With Self**

Working out your internal alignment is one of the biggest keys to dealing with leadership fatigue and what you can do to help yourself as a leader.

2. **Redefine Success for Yourself**

Getting clear on YOUR vision for success, purpose that drives you and values you live by, are foundational to building a business on your own terms.

3. **Listen And Trust Yourself**

This takes work, but you must do YOU. Always practice self-care.

4. **Surround Yourself With People Who Support You ...**

...and share your same values. Kindly remove or use strong boundaries around everyone else.

5. **Set Boundaries**

Look to set boundaries in all aspects of your life and business. This powerful tool is the key to increasing your capacity for success.

6. **Know Your Numbers**

Fall in love with your numbers and they will fall in love with you. Learn the story and drivers behind your financial statements and align everything in your business back to your numbers.

7. **Get Good Advice**

Seek out those experts who can provide great insight and foresight based on things that are important to you. Take ownership and ensure you understand their advice.

8. **Master having difficult conversations**

Learning this skill with kindness is a superpower.

9. **Hire A Good Coach**

Hold yourself accountable to a great mentor or coach who has walked in your shoes. They are invaluable for helping you set your strategies for growth, navigate challenges, and reflect on any blind spots.

10. **Do The Work**

No explanation required!

ABOUT THE AUTHOR

SAM DEAN

Sam Dean is a serial Founder, Entrepreneur, Growth Advisor, Speaker, and Podcaster.

In the past ten years, she has worked with hundreds of driven experts and professionals having been one herself for over 25 years. These are highly educated women and men who got into professions they believed would bring them stability and prosperity. Now more than ever they're working more hours than they thought humanly possible and making nowhere near the money they thought they would, feeling completely trapped. Their profession has become a prison and they are suffering from Leadership Fatigue Syndrome.

They think the problem is about lack of time, resources and know how or that technology is the answer. But we know the real problem is solving the fatigue issue, in which we need to focus internally. Without this shift we simply don't have the energy to lead the required change to build the businesses we want.

The **BlueprintHQ** programs Sam's designed, helps leaders to overcome fatigue and build scalable systems and networks, create working cultures no one wants to leave, quit trading hours for dollars and establish success on their own terms.

Check out her podcast **Business Habitat** on your favourite podcast app, where conversations are had about building business habitats that align with their leaders.

Connect with Sam on Social Media:

LinkedIn for BlueprintHQ –

https://www.linkedin.com/company/blueprinthq

Podcast for BlueprintHQ –

https://www.blueprinthq.com.au/podcast

- facebook.com/bprinthq
- instagram.com/blueprinthq_australia
- linkedin.com/in/samdean13

6
TWO BENT RODS

by SAM BECKMAN

HEY, I'm Sam and I grew up in Ipswich, was painfully shy regarding speaking to anyone, but would always give things a go.

Mum and Dad always took me fishing, I don't remember a time when I didn't fish as kid. I loved the outdoors and camping, running, and reading. I remember getting horribly sunburnt. By the time I was aged 8 or 9 I'd say to Dad, that I was going to be a fisherwoman when I grew up. My little brother came along and started going fishing with Dad and by age 13 I had other interests and now I wanted a motorbike.

I'd grown up with riding my next-door neighbour's minibike. Mum and Dad said yes, but I'd have to get a job and they'd go me halves if I saved enough money. So, I did and in no time, I had my Honda XL 100 complete with blinkers and headlights. I was so little, and it was so heavy, but I would ride it out in the bush around Blackstone and Bundamba and along with my brother and cousin ride along what is now the Cunningham Highway, all the way out to Purga.

There was one trip, the three of us were sorting of racing our parents to our other cousin's place. Adults on the road, kids through the bush. While we were scooting along the highway, it was being built, the odd truck would be there. My brother had a little minibike, and no matter how much he pulled back on the throttle he couldn't go any faster. There was a huge truck looming down on him, the driver was laughing, he could have just driven right over the top of him. Then we'd ride out to Sellars where there were sheer drop offs to ride down, scary but fun.

When family came over the men would be playing cards for money, I quickly learned the games and would sometimes sit in for dad. He also taught me to play table tennis, I have a mean serve which few people can return. I played darts and I played a lot of pool.

I did do more feminine things with my Mum and Nanny, learning to do needlework and knitting. By the time I was aged 12 or 13 I would knit my own patterned jumpers.

I've always had a tenacious attitude. When I was learning to play pool seriously, I would just keep at it. I lost nearly every game for well over a year. Then slowly but surely the tide began to turn. I'm not the best, but I could hold my own with the boys. I would play against my grandfather, who would annoyingly and playfully cheat and try to make it nearly impossible for me to hit any of my balls. It only served to make me better. I can get out of most snooker shots. The more an obstacle is put in my way, the harder I will try to find a way out, or to think outside of the box.

After I left school, I trained as a typesetter, this position is nearly obsolete nowadays. Desktop publishing can now be done by anyone. When I learnt, fonts were very limited and they were made from glass, looked like a glass saucepan lid, only flat. Geez, I'm sounding old, I'm 52 at time of writing. I was one of the first people in SE Qld to be trained on Apple Macs. This would turn out to be my first step into business. Setting up artwork layout for various projects, I worked inside of my father's printing business, doing work for him as well as myself. At one point, I was being flown in to teach other companies how to use programs such as PageMaker and QuarkXPress. I was all over the technology. I ended up selling it as part of Dad's business when he sold. I've worked in universities, alongside graphic artists, small and large newspapers, and boutique agencies. I was good at what I did; I can type 100wpm with near perfect accuracy so could get work done quickly. I would walk into any job interview, expecting I would walk out with the job, my confidence in myself and my abilities were very high. Oh, and most times, I would get the job.

Fast forward to today, I've been married to my husband Jeremy for 21 years, have three children, one lovely granddaughter, Lilly, and another on the way.

2 Bent Rods is a business Jeremy and I founded together; it is based in Victoria Point in the Redlands in a lovely seaside community in South East Queensland. Our classes run from the Gold Coast, Brisbane to the Sunshine Coast and plenty of suburbs in between. *2 Bent Rods* was born in 2004 after a day at the beach with our family. Jeremy and I were taking our kids fishing, aged 2, 3 and 9 years at the time.

We took them to Wellington Point for a day of bait gathering and fishing. We started pumping yabbies with the kids and other kids started joining in and wanting to have a go. It wasn't long before we had a hoard of kids following us around and asking questions. Many of them had never seen a yabby before. After we had collected enough yabbies to use for bait, we then went bait netting. We were catching heaps of creatures in the net from toadfish, juvenile whiting, flathead, bream and even stingrays and shovel nose sharks. The hoard of kids had grown to around 20 by now and my husband and I found ourselves explaining all that we caught to them.

We let them have a quick pat – even the stingray and shovel nose, the kids were so excited. Then they helped us to release the other fish that were safe to touch, and we released everything else that we weren't going to use for bait. Then we went fishing. I can't remember if we caught a fish, I was just amazed that the kids that lived so close to the beach and used the beach, didn't really know anything about the beach or the marine life that inhabited it. My husband and I couldn't let it go, so made a few enquiries and asked for a meeting with Bruce Alvey – a Queensland icon in the fishing industry. We put our idea forward and asked his advice. We then asked if we could come to an arrangement to pay off some rods and reels, which he agreed to.

Having a young family and my husband having to have his lower back fused only a year before, we were both receiving Centrelink benefits, so had no savings.

The birth of *2 Bent Rods*. We worked on some lesson plans which were very flexible and open to change. Classes were structured so the kids learnt not only about fishing but also the marine environment, fishing, personal and marine safety, as well as sustainability. The classes had to be fun as well as educational, to help kids get off their devices, make new friends and enjoy what our great outdoors lifestyle has to offer. There are so many benefits to going fishing, apart from being outside in the sunshine. Fitness, healthy eating, a love for the environment, fine motor skills, patience, sustainable practices, mental health, a love of the ocean and respect for rules and an understanding of why we need to have some regulations in place. They get to understand firsthand why we need to be sustainable and not keep every fish we catch for the sake of it. They also learn about rubbish and its effect on nature and the animals and sea life. It's not just about fishing.

Armed with our rods, we went and sat at local beaches ready to give lessons. We didn't get any customers! This was before Facebook and just as the internet was starting. I hadn't done any courses in marketing but did retain a bit of information from when I was typing up marketing and sales manuals back when I was younger. All I knew was you had to keep going. Get on the phone and ask. The worst they can say is NO!

I started contacting local newspapers and they started to come on board, running articles and putting us in the what's on sections. By 2008, *2 Bent Rods* was contracting to Brisbane City Councils Active and Healthy program, offering free and low-cost classes to their residents. This then expanded to include Ipswich, Logan and Moreton Bay Councils. We are still currently working with them and are preferred suppliers and have current contracts running 6 to 9 months in advance.

That same year, we also started the Kids Marine Zone. We were contracted by the local radio station 4BC to run kids' activities at the Tinnie and Tackle Show. We ran the weekend for a pittance, and they tucked us up an alleyway as they were worried how it would go. So, were we? Parents were able to drop the kids off to do the activities while they walked peacefully around the show, thus freeing them up to talk to salespeople and hopefully make large sales.

It was very successful and Marine Safety Queensland then contracted us directly to run the zones at their shows, even in other parts of Queensland, including Mackay. The events manager took us under his wing and taught me about charging what you are worth. Within a couple of years, we were charging 10 times more than at our very first event. We ran these shows up to 3 times a year for around 7 years and it grew to being 30% of our business. We were devastated when they dissolved, and the new entity didn't want to continue with our services. This taught me about having our eggs in one basket and we now have multiple income streams from varying lessons and products.

At our Kids Marine Zone, we would be given prime space, sometimes in weird shapes, so we could entertain hundreds of kids each day. Our busiest day was when we had around 800 kids come through. We were a show in a show. Kids would work their way around the various stations, we had large round tanks with live creatures. Everything from bream, to stingray, stonefish, occasionally even small sharks.

There was yabby pumping, rod casting, craft, lure painting, knot tying, and mullet chukka activities for the kids to do. We would only have 3 to 4 days before a show to go and catch all the creatures for the tank. So, each year we had different creatures, from live mud crabs to spanner crabs and large flathead. I had built up great relationships with all the major fishing manufacturers and they would donate hundreds of prizes for the kids.

Over the years, they have dropped off as we wear them out with the sheer volume of kids that come through our programs.

From this we started a mini Kids Marine Zone to take to the vacation care centres over school holidays and then started to run excursions as well. We now regularly book out and always have forward bookings for the next holidays. This has built up to anywhere from 800- 1300 kids over a two-week holiday period.

In 2009 we started classes fishing for carp and learning about pest fish.

By 2011 we had run our first pest fishing for tilapia for Moreton Bay Council, educating the public on the detrimental effects these fish were having on our waterways and to our native species.

In 2015 we started pest fishing event management – being a one stop shop for Councils and corporates to organise a family friendly pest fishing competition which helps them meet their General Biosecurity Obligations.

In 2017 we tested the market for fishing school – a term time after-school activity, where kids received their own rod and reel and other tackle as well as weekly lessons. Although reasonably popular we need to work on it more and have appropriate manufacturers and sponsors in place for it to work properly. This has been shelved for the time being.

I've been in business a long time, but it hasn't been easy. We have had some great highs but some of the lows, I suppose you call them character building. There's been times when we couldn't afford the electricity and had to borrow a generator for the lights and live out of an esky for weeks, this isn't easy at any time, let alone with three young kids. We still had a roof over our heads though. Around the same time, we defaulted on our car loan and while I was out doing the shopping, found a debt collector at my car, he was there to repossess it. A lot of quick talking and tears and I was able to keep my car for another day to try to come up with the funds, which we borrowed from my parents.

2 Bent Rods has been run from various rental houses all over South East Queensland, even remotely from the Gladstone area for a couple of years. This wasn't easy. There were plenty of times I had to jump in the car for a quick 7-hour journey to cover staff and sort out any problems. I slowed the business down while we were up there 2013-2015. My Mum had been diagnosed with cancer not long after we moved and she died in March 2015, two days after my Dad's 70th. Mum was only 67. Her death absolutely rocked my world. I was thankful I spent the last month with her but regret not talking about the serious stuff.

The kids were left mostly unsupervised and had to get themselves off to school as Jeremy was working 14 hour days, although they were at an age where they were able to fend for themselves. They started to play up and get into trouble. Looking back, I don't think I took their grief into account. My grief turned into, I'm not sure what you'd call it. I could hardly function; I lost control of the kids and could consistently be found in the corner of the bathroom or even on the floor in the shower sobbing uncontrollably. I needed help from friends and the school to get the kids to go to school.

A few months after Mum passed, we moved back to Brisbane. We stayed at my cousin's place and couldn't find a house to rent, we kept getting knocked back. We ended up homeless, living in a camper trailer over summer in the hot Queensland sun. It was horrible, embarrassing and all those sorts of feels. I've never felt so useless or worthless before. If it wasn't for my cousin letting us stay there, I'm not sure where we would be.

We finally got accepted for a house and I came across a scholarship application for a business school, I applied and won it. For the next 6 months I learnt so much, met so many other women in business and was gob smacked they genuinely wanted to see other women succeed. For the past 12 years I had been on my own, no networking as such, never went to in person events. I didn't know there were groups where women lifted each other up and with a lot of happiness to share their knowledge. During the course I met Michelle and completed a program about money and learned about the universe and the laws of attraction. Since then, my confidence has picked up no end. Although we were still on the bones of our bums, I started to go to events and meet people.

I entered my first awards - What's On 4 Kids Awards which also gave me tickets to their conference, where I met so many people in the kid's activity business. This is the first time I had thought of the business as something other than being in the fishing industry. I made it to the finals. I didn't really think much of it as I had the mindset, "every child wins a prize". I just figured everyone made it through to the finals (and I still do to some degree).

Earlier in the day, while we were getting ready to have lunch, I saw a lady in the foyer crying, so I gave her a cuddle, chatted with her, and hopefully cheered her up. At the end of the conference, everyone left to go to their hotel rooms, to shower and change and get their hair and make up done. I couldn't do that as we couldn't afford it. While everyone was getting ready, I was sitting on a bus stop bench bawling my eyes out, feeling sorry for myself, wanting someone to give me a cuddle. That wasn't going to happen on a dark street in the valley, more than likely, I'd get mugged! So, I got up and went into the public toilets to try to doll myself up for the night.

I was amazed when we won the Best Kids School Holiday activity. It was so exciting, I got up on stage, to say a few words, that I'd worked out before hand, thanked the sponsors, started on my speech, and looked up and went blank. I said something lame, like, "I'm too nervous for this! Keep your kids fishing!" and walked off the stage. Jeremy picked me up not long after, I felt a little like Cinderella, having to leave the ball early. Truth be known we didn't have the spare money for me to Uber it. In 2019 we backed the win up, this time beating Australia Zoo and Australian Rugby, it made me so proud to think our little business could be considered worthy of being in the same categories as these icons. 2021 and we cleaned up winning 2 Gold and 2 Runner Ups.

Still in 2017, I started to apply what I was learning in the business school to *2 Bent Rods* and slowly but surely more work started coming in. The following year, I found the money for a business coach for 3 months. It wasn't cheap, she gave me so much work to do, picked apart my website and basically said I didn't have a business, I had a hobby.

I did get offended, really offended ... but ... a few months later I really looked at our turnover, costs and how I was running it and thought, "She's right!" I needed to do something. I was also so stressed out because I hadn't put any tax returns in for years and owed the Taxation Department so much money. I finally pulled my head out of the sand and rang them to face the music. I said, I owe a heap of money and want to try to sort it out. He said he'd check and then said, you don't owe us anything. I said I think you're mistaken, check deeper because I definitely owe money. His next comment left me in absolute awe – yes, I can see you did owe us, we have decided to defer all fees as long as you keep up to date and make all payments on time from here on in. Needless to say, I'm always on time and totally update. If I ever default, they have an option to raise the debt again. The amount of relief and stress lifted was enormous.

I then started working with a new coach who was more my pace and started to build the business back up again. We revamped some of the programs and tweaked existing ones. Then we looked at staffing issues, we were so run down from doing everything ourselves. I would do the classes as well as social media, accounts, bookings etc., same as any business owner wearing all the hats, but you need to be careful you don't wear too many that they stifle you.

I've had 2 staff members with us for nearly 10 years.

Both boys came to lessons when they were around 12 and over the years they would help at various classes and events. One is now a teacher and still works with us over the holidays and the other works most weekends and school holidays. The same with 4 or 5 more staff, they have all either had lessons or a birthday party with us when they were younger. Their memory of *2 Bent Rods* is of a fun place and to most of them, it was their dream job. I find that so endearing and it makes my heart swell. It's hard to keep staff when you're a seasonal business. I have been lucky these guys have been with us so long and I know I will miss them all greatly when they leave to follow their career paths.

I think where our team culture would differ from a lot of other businesses is that we have watched these kids grow up. Over the years we have become friends with their parents and know each other by sight and name and attend the odd function together. We know when the kids get their drivers licence, we don't have them for much longer. We try to have them ready to run/supervise some of the classes by this point.

Now they are mobile, they can pick up any gear needed and do a lot more classes. If they feel they are capable, I'm happy to give them the reins for some of the classes to see how they go. This is why I try to get them speaking at the classes as early as possible. They can then start to help train the new lot of staff that will come through. I know our original 5 staff will be back on and off over their lifetime, in between jobs, looking to earn a bit extra coin because that's how family works, and they have been a fantastic working family over the years.

In January 2020, our first class of international students was cancelled due to Covid 19. By the end of March, we had ceased all classes. I personally took it hard for about a month, before deciding to take the opportunity to review our business to see how we could add even more value.

We were able to keep one out of 6 staff employed and created new educational tools for the business. The downturn also allowed us to research and create a couple of new income streams for the business. Due to covid restrictions, we were allowed to run 1:1 classes, so we worked out lesson plans and found them to be very popular. It started off with adults taking up the offer, but as restrictions lifted it was mainly father and sons wanting to book in.

Our pest fishing events have a 3-tier attack on pest species:

- Public education
- Community participation in fishing competitions targeting adult pest fish
- Restocking with native fish

We've been trying to position the business to provide a commercial service in pest control to government authorities and other organization's responsible for the management of our waterways. It will also help us to collect evidence-based data to assist state and local government authorities in biosecurity management. This will in part include a major state-wide pest fishing competition with heats throughout Queensland and targeted to families. I'm hoping to turn it into a yearly Pest Fishing Trail that also has Heats in rural areas.

Our staff levels have increased to 12 casuals and 2 school-based office trainees…both these boys are on the spectrum and will be doing a Certificate III in Office Administration.

Part way through 2021 we were accepted as a tourism business which saw us gain new customers with each of their promotions to help stimulate the tourism industry. These listings mean we are seen by both local and state government tourism departments, and I believe this has definitely put more eyes on our business.

People book private lessons for their families, and we will offer fish/creature specific classes e.g., squidding, surf fishing, crabbing etc., customers are able to choose their instructor and we've opened our website to other fishing guides and charters to advertise their services.

Due to local, state, and federal grants, I've been able to keep moving forward. Some of the grants meant website, branding, social media strategies, business coaching etc., could all be purchased. One of the grants was for two fishing buggies and ramps to connect to the back of our car, to make it easier to travel with the equipment. These were made and the number of mistakes, lack of quality finish with sharp edges that could hurt the kids was unbelievable. The business owner has dismissed me, probably thinking I will go away quietly. But I won't. I was going to just get it fixed by someone else, but that's not fair. I shouldn't have to pay for someone else's cock ups. So, I will follow it as far as I can to get a ruling, if that means I must go to court, so be it. It's so disappointing to have the buggies there not in use, while we are manually humping all the gear to and from the beach. So frustrating.

On an average year, *2 Bent Rods* will run around 200 events, most small but still similar manpower to set them up. I'm the queen of cancellations. With all the Covid related shutdowns, bad weather etc., I have streamlined cancelling events to a fine art. I try to have it run seamlessly from having new dates and venues ready to go for corporate and having new dates and tickets set up, stakeholders notified, before any customers know we have had any dramas. I like to have all the options available to inconvenience the end user as little as possible.

We have applied for a Citizen Science Grant to help get word out about our app. Through another grant and sponsorship, we were able to get our own branded app. This is available for anyone to use and is free. It works in a couple of ways. Individuals can take a photo of their fish on a measuring device, select the species, how it was caught, rod, net, what bait, lure was used as well as location throughout Australia.

The app can also be used to take registration and payments for the fishing competitions we run. People upload their fish, which is checked in the background for correct measurements, uploads the fish to the live leader board so everyone can see using the app during competitions. This cuts down on errors at weigh in and the time competitors need to wait for the presentation of prizes and the winners announced.

In the back end, marine specialists check all the fish and creatures that have been uploaded. Not only for size but also for any trauma. They can investigate if it is locational or human error and if a course of action can be taken. Because we will also be keeping records for everything, we catch in all our classes, we will get a good understanding of the juvenile species locations and timings.

I'll leave you with a couple of stories. The first is Alice, she was 2 years old. We were running a class at Nudgee Beach, and we had caught a male crab. We showed everyone how to tell it was a boy. It has a pointed triangle on its belly. Alice's Dad said to her, "Boy, pointed triangle, penis, boy." I shook my head and said, "We don't need to go there."

Then Alice went off fishing, the tide was about 100m out and I was coming back from a break. Little Alice is running towards me with her hand stretched out, yelling at the top of her lungs. "Sam, Sam, look what I caught. Look, it's a boy, it's got a penis!" I laughed so hard,

I nearly spat out my teeth (I've had false teeth since I was 24 years old but that's a nightmare story for another time). Alice had caught a reasonable sized toadfish; she was clutching it so tight that poop was coming out of its bum.

A few years later a lady rings to book in a little girl, I recognised the name and I said to her, "Alice has been before." Her mother said, yes but that was years ago. I told her the story and she said, "Yes, that was Alice. I'm so surprised you remember!" I told her I will never forget Alice.

Another year, we were doing a class at Brighton and a man, and his carer stopped to watch us. The man had an ABI (Acquired Brain Injury) and wasn't good on uneven ground. We asked if he wanted to have a turn. He climbed over the little rock wall and walked over the soft sand to take control of the rod. His carer was a bit concerned as he couldn't find the man's toy car, that was never out of his hands or sight. He had put it away in his pocket. The joy and excitement on the man's face is one I will never forget. It is a great feeling knowing we have eased someone's pain or given them some respite, even if just for a couple of minutes. Some of those feelings will stay with them (and us) for a lifetime.

If you were thinking of starting a business, I would say… do your research. Ask yourself a couple of questions such as why do you want to start a business? Is it to create a job for yourself? Do you have a cause? Do you want to save the world? Really home in on what you want to do, find out if there is anyone already in that space and follow them, see what they are doing, what seems to be working for them? Where can you see them fall down? This is where you can base your point of difference.

Don't be afraid to reach out for help. Fail fast. This one is easier said than done. Find the parts of the business you really don't want to do and outsource them, whether that is to a partner, employee, VA (Virtual Assistant), or another business. Celebrate all the wins, not just the big ones. Don't be afraid to put yourself out there. Connect and network, at the very least you will come away with some amazing friends.

I still have big expansion plans for *2 Bent Rods*, including a range of fishing shirts that should be available next year and gradually will be adding fishing products. As I'm getting older, I need to think more about residual income and getting off the tools, so to speak. A children's book is also on the cards. Find a job you love, and you will never work a day in your life. I have that, this is what was put here to do. This is my soul's purpose.

BUSINESS TIPS FOR ENTREPRENEURS:

Tip 1

FWOT! Quite simply, *forget what others think*! You're not taking the chance to build your own business so you can sit inside your head with all the negative brain chatter dragging you down. You're running your own game, so do it your way. Don't listen to how others think you should do things or take advice from "experts" or naysayers who tell you you're wrong. The best businesses are built by people who are wildly passionate about their own vision and don't let others tell them otherwise. If Elon Musk and Jeff Bezos can incorporate space travel into their plans, you can too!

Tip 2

Surround yourself with like-minded people. You don't have to fit in. Dr Suess said it best when he said, "Why fit in when you were born to stand out?" Chances are there are others just like you, find them. Having a crew of incredible people around you can be the catalyst in surviving the wild business journey. There's no point in being in a room full of wallflowers if you're a wildcat! Just like there's no point being in a room full of ego-preneurs if you're mostly holistic and down to earth. Find a crew that lifts you up, keeps you motivated and allows you to be truly yourself.

Tip 3

Burn out is a BITCH! So, make sure you take care of yourself along the way. You don't have to do all the things all the time. You're well within your right as a budding entrepreneur building your own business to take some time out with NO apologies. No one will die if you don't reply to an email within a minute of it hitting your Inbox. Be sure to schedule time out for you. Trust me, this one is important!

Tip 4

There's never a perfect time, so just do it. Throw mud at the wall and see if it sticks, take the risk, make a move. Waiting for the right time, perfect presentation or trying to read trends will see you left at the gate while everyone else is running forward. You don't have to wait for everything to come together. You'll never have a better time when you're running your own business to try things. Some will flop, some might be gold. Be brave enough to gamble on your own ideas, be creative. You may just find it's the best move you make!

Tip 5

Don't quit your day job! Read that again. The biggest mistake budding business owners make is walking out on a perfectly good pay cheque to pursue their grand ideas in business only to realise 5 minutes down the road they don't have the cash-flow to support the ideas. I worked on building my business while I worked for someone else, this gave me the financial stability I needed to pursue the business without the risk of going broke! You might think you have a million-dollar idea, but an idea untested and not supported is bound to go bust! You may not have to stay in a full-time job, but my advice is to always make sure you are ready to take the leap into a business venture understanding all your costs, outlay and cash-flow needs. You can build a wildly successful business with a few hours of dedication a week and when you know you can support the business growth and cover off that income for yourself, then you're truly free to tell the boss you're out!

Tip 6

Find a healthy work-life balance because it really does go too quick! The biggest trap in business and pursuing all of those BIG dreams is sometimes we make it our ONLY focus! It's a trap! There's nothing appealing about working a gazillion hours a week in your business when everything else around you turns to shit. There's not enough money in the world to replace your time here on earth, so don't confuse it as your #1 priority. Make time for relationships important to you, hobbies that keep you creative and curious and for your health and wellbeing. Make it a non-negotiable, unwavering part of your business plan from the beginning and you'll truly know success.

Tip 7

Focus on profit, not revenue. I've met many a business owner over the years that will brag openly and loudly about their turnover in their business, yet they pay themselves pennies on the dime. Ain't nobody got time for that. You're not working in a business to make huge revenue and at the end of the day be a penniless pauper, you want the money honey! So, focus on profit, not your revenue. While I'm on this point, it's a great idea to sit with a financial guru to work out your financial goals and how to best make every dollar work for you. Everyone has a different situation going on and I'm definitely not qualified to give financial advice, so I'll merely say seek it!

Tip 8

Choose your battles wisely. I have a saying that I use with my mentoring clients as it helps them visualise this point. When starting out and growing your business, you might want to do everything, but you'll be limited, perhaps by time, money, resources, or knowledge. It makes absolutely no sense in trying to do them all, because you'll only make a mess of things. Picture eating a watermelon. You can't eat an entire watermelon all at once; I'd like to see you try, but I do feel this is physically impossible for a human. What you can do is chunk it down and eat it, bit by bit. Focus on each bite, knowing you can take it in, chomp it down, swallow and go again. Business is the same. You need to focus on each step and do it well, each small step is another move forward.

Tip 9

Eat the damn frog! And I'm not talking about those delicious Cadbury Freddo ones. I'm talking about getting the biggest, most obnoxious, tedious tasks off your to-do list done and dusted. We all have them, and we like to avoid them…but they'll still be there tomorrow, getting louder and louder. They'll stop you sleeping, make you restless, obstruct your focus and make you crazy. Just get them done. Once you've eaten that big fat frog, you'll be free from the weight and ready to chomp down the next one!

Tip 10

Stop watching your competition! Ever tried to run a race while you're focused on the person running against you? Chances are you'll either fall flat on your face or they'll run straight past you. You can't focus on moving forward while you're looking in another direction. This is a hard one for business owners to hear, as it's so easy to be curious about what others are doing in their businesses, particularly if that business appears to be more successful than your own. Try a different angle. If you do find yourself curious about what your competition are doing, take it from an analytical point of view and find a gap in what they could be doing better – that's your opportunity for a point of difference right there. There's always a better play, so find it and run with that!

Tip 11

Break the rules! I'm supposed to give you my top 10 Tips but I'm giving you 11 because if you don't push the boundaries a little bit then you'll always stay mediocre and who wants to do that? And in case no one has told you today, you're a bloody rockstar! There are so many people in life that don't take the chance on themselves. If you're one of the brave ones, who dared to pursue a life and business of your own, then more power to you! It takes guts, dedication, determination, and self-belief to start. Even though at times, you'll let that little voice inside try to tell you otherwise, here you are daring to follow your dream and that makes you awesome! Any time you need to be reminded of that, you can come back here and read that again.

Tip 12

Identify a Problem: Look for a problem or need in the market that you can solve with your product or service. Successful businesses are built on providing solutions to real problems.

Tip 13

Market Research: Conduct thorough market research to understand your target audience, competition, and industry trends.

Tip 14

Create a Business Plan: Develop a comprehensive business plan that outlines your goals, target market, marketing strategies, financial projections, and operational details. This will serve as your roadmap and help you stay focussed.

Tip 15

Build a strong team: Surround yourself with talented individuals who complement your skills and share your vision. Hiring the right people and delegating tasks effectively is crucial for business growth.

Tip 16

Customer Focus: Put your customers at the centre of your business. Understand their needs, provide exceptional customer service, and continuously seek feedback to improve your products or services.

Go get 'em!

7
FREEDOM & CHOICE

by Co-Author: MR. JEAN-MARCEL ELIÉZER MALLIATÉ MDR

I **was** not born under a swinging palm tree near the magnificent blue ocean shore of the pearl of the Indian Ocean, L'ile de Maurice, but in the capital's hospital Port Louis.

I was born in Mauritius, the first-born son of Jacques and Odile and enjoyed my life at school, run by extremely strict nuns. I had many friends and was encouraged to study hard.

My parents worked in England for 3 months, and we lived with our grandparents. During their absence, my brother and I faced bullying by one of my uncles. My grandparents and aunts were nurturing, protective and provided a sanctuary and safe zone for us.

At nine years of age, a family member sexually abused me one night when my parents had gone out. They had come home unexpectedly and found her abusing me. My mother slapped her, and I ran to my bedroom, this incident was never mentioned again. I have only spoken about it with my brother, still to this day. My sexual predator is still in my life and has attended family functions over the years.

As a result of this incident, I chose to work in the field of child protection and mediation to support families in crisis in the best interest of their children.

I lived in Mauritius until my family moved to Australia in 1967, a country beginning to free itself from its White Australian policy, and I was without any basic English to help me adapt quickly. Speaking only

French, it was easy to improve my language skills as my mother was at Cambridge University as a trained teacher of French, Latin, and English at a girls' school and my father worked for the Taxation Department. We began our primary schooling at Ramsgate Public School, with great kindness and understanding shown by Ms Howard, our teacher, and Deputy Principal.

On the first day during lunch, five boys bullied me shaping up for a fight and name calling, pushing, and shoving. They thought I was an Aboriginal person and called me "boong" and "fuzzy wuzzy," a fight began, fists were flying, and three teachers were very quick to break it up, as other students cheered on. "Fight, fight, fight!"

After school, the boys followed my brother and I home and continued to bully us. Outnumbered, we felt like we were in a war zone with no escape and no friends.

Homesick, desperate, and bullied, we returned to school each day feeling like we did not belong. I struggled accepting my new home, feeling rejection, and dealing with the bullies became an obsession of survival. Ms Howard spent a lot of her time helping me learn about Australian culture, reassuring me that this was a great school and that I would soon fit in, and encouraged me to play Rugby League.

There were more fights to come, and Rugby League was a great outlet. My friend Peter often came to our house to escape his father, who was a chronic alcoholic and abusive towards his mother and sister. When Peter defended them, his father would also beat him up and he became traumatised. He became so troubled; he ended his life at the young age of seventeen. This devastated me as I could not help him battle his demons, we were only in high school.

My primary school girlfriend Julie became the dux of the school and was also bullied mercilessly due to her obesity. Julie became anorexic and lost her will to live, also cutting her life short in high school. I wasn't equipped then as I am now, with the skills that could have helped both my friends.

Although I'm a Mediator, I am also a trained Counsellor, and it was the influence of my two best friends' inability to cope with their situations, early in my life, that led me on the pathway to my chosen career.

This sadness prevailed for quite some time and was compounded with the news that Peter had jumped off Australia Square with a note tied to his neck reading, "God gave me permission to die." I lost both my dearest friends to suicide in high school.

I was devastated by the loss of my friends who meant so much to me from an early age, now gone forever, like the many friends I had in Mauritius, gone forever. As a young person, many questions came up for me, as the reality of life and death became cloudy and the purpose in my life blurred.

Years later, I married and relocated to Perth with our baby son, leaving Sydney behind. Life was good and two years later our beautiful daughter arrived, another blessing, a welcome joy to our family's lives. Our marriage lasted thirteen years ending in a legal battle for custody.

The Family Law system was quite different then, using a "fault system" of blame which resulted in bitter fights in court, with lawyers destroying our life savings and loss of our marital home. This caused disharmony and ongoing conflict in our co-parenting relationship which had significant long-term effects.

We relocated to Sydney to save our marriage but were unable to, so I chose to leave the marital home. This resulted in the costly and lengthy process of litigation.

After several months, the conflict escalated and payments were neglected on our beautiful family home in Oyster Bay, the two cars and bankruptcy resulted as legal costs mounted. We became bitter as we did not have the skills to communicate as co-parents, destroyed by lawyers and we finally lost everything. As time went on there were many excuses preventing me from seeing my children.

Our litigation matter resulted in my inability to see my son for four years and daughter for thirteen years! Litigation took my home, business, cars, and children from my life, after having worked so hard since I was 17 years of age.

I saved my earnings diligently throughout my career, believing I had chosen the right girl from my church to marry. I was happily married for thirteen years and had known her for four years before marriage and was now plunged into desperation and disappeared overseas to escape.

I became depressed and angry finding solace in new relationships, creating negative reactions with my ex-wife and her new husband. I was told that my children did not want to see me or my parents and this was a devastating blow. I realised that I had ignored my children and not provided for their needs, destroying the relationship we had together which contributed to its demise.

Eventually our son decided to contact me when he turned eighteen and by that stage, I had studied psychology and Dispute Resolution. Lunch with my newfound son was intense and I was asked to just listen. I heard his story and shed tears of sadness, as well as joy, finally feeling love again from my first born.

Unfortunately, my daughter chose not to contact me until she turned twenty-one. The pain was immense, and the guilt was always there, but I continued to build my relationship with her slowly through my son, until she finally reconnected with me.

My family values helped me immensely when dealing with adversities, preventing loss of hope and my self-worth. Re-education in the fields of Social Science, Counselling and Dispute Resolution helped me gain an understanding of my own contribution to the many discords in my life. By facing the traumas, descending into the depths of clinical depression was averted through my own use of counselling and family support.

I avoided my parental responsibilities and the mental anguish of being exiled from my children became overwhelming. I viewed the defeat of child custody as sanctioned by the judge, instigated by their mother and her legal counsel. It had been a win/lose outcome, and I knew how much I had lost. Thankfully my parents and family remained in my corner and several months later, they wished me bon voyage as I flew to Fiji.

I met the tall, elegant daughter of a Levuka village chief and found myself married a second time, celebrating a traditional Fijian wedding in grass skirts.

Unfortunately, it was a short-lived marriage and we separated in Dublin, each going our own way. Upon my return to Australia, my mother encouraged me to extend my understanding of relationships and the importance of good communication and conflict resolution. I knew that I needed to re-educate myself to make better choices to improve my life, as I faced being single again. I was missing my children and found that female companionship was not the answer. My mother suggested I study Social Science which included Human Behaviour and Psychology. After many years of study, I graduated with Masters of Dispute Resolution, from the University of Technology Sydney's Law Faculty.

Equipped with a toolbox of skills and a new professional career, life had improved. I began to help others with conflict resolution, working with separated parents who required my help with Parenting Plans and assistance in dividing their assets. I worked with many community organisations, corporate and government agencies in different roles mediating and training others how to resolve their issues in a peaceful way. I became adept at assisting separated parents to create Parenting Plans and Financial Agreements that were in the best interests of their children.

The knowledge and insight I gained from my own personal experiences in Family Court, helped me to support parents in the separation process. What I learned through my own situation, gave me the ability to help parents struggling with financial issues, emotional wellbeing and to focus on their co-parenting responsibilities.

I observed many parents who were excluded from their children's lives growing up; become depressed, suicidal, self-harming and even committing grievous crimes against their once loving families.

The Family Law Act of 1975 became focused on the best interest of the child, family law mediation became compulsory as it was proven to be more effective in enabling parents and grandparents to have access to their children in a co-parenting style.

Mediation helps to relieve the overwhelming pain caused by parental separation and conflict through litigation as children are forced to take sides. When working as a Family Dispute Resolution Practitioner FDRP Family Law Mediator, my role was to assist parents to focus on their children's needs, express their emotions and feelings to each other. They always gained a better understanding of each other as parents, recognising their partner relationship was finished but their co-parenting relationship continued until they die.

In my role as a FDRP, I apply advanced verbal communication and interpersonal skills, tailoring my approach to suit multi-cultural parties and sometimes requesting the assistance of a co-mediator for gender balance when dealing with complex cases.

Through my work, I'm known as an effective, analytical thinker. I always show empathy for parents as this comes naturally to me due to my personal experiences.

I invite you the visit my website where you can find my business details:
InterMEDIATE Dispute Management:
www.InvestigationandMediation.com.au

In our Mediation and Family Dispute Resolution FDR, we offer face-to-face services and virtual mediation, in 'a solo and co' model which is highly suited for high conflict parties available across Australia and beyond.

Parents are helped to craft robust agreements they can live with and in the best interests of their children. We begin with a confidential Initial Assessment, to help parents prepare and determine their suitability for the FDR process.

We help support parents trapped living under the same roof whilst trying to separate their lives. FDR assists them to reduce the intense pressure as they navigate around each other, regularly spilling out insults, blame and hurling accusations at each other, often in front of their children, scaring the children and further inflaming the situation.

Our team helps separating parents to avoid the process of litigation. FDR uses a tried-and-true process to reduce increased marital and parenting tension, frustration, anger and even violence. Our parties contact us directly as Family Courts are backed up with thousands of cases. Community organisations have long waiting lists for separated parents trying to find their way to resolution, only to get lawyers charging huge fees for writing letters of demand to the other side.

These are costly legal services to separated parents who often are being charged by the minute for photocopies, phone calls and emails knowingly at an exorbitant rate. They have lost the choice and continue to rely on the lawyer's ability to negotiate and give up their own voices.

Neglecting the need to improve their parental communication and relationships as separated parents at this crucial time, creates the worst memories for their children. Their faith on the outcome through this legal pathway is cemented by the amount of money they deposit in the lawyer's trust account at the beginning of their unknown litigious journey. They know further funding will be required as the letters, applications and injunctions sought continue to be exchanged. Plunged into heated telephone conversations with the ex, hosted by lawyers, clock ticking, and money flushed down the drain, costing a fortune; never to be discussed again.

When the impending court day comes, a barrister is often required as the lawyer needs their expertise to support the groundwork, fuelling the fire and obtaining a decision in favour of their client. The judge looks up, sees the statue of Lady Justice, and fixates on the sword she is holding. He chops off the head of one legal representative before him and awards what seems to the other side, a court decision masked as a fair outcome. A Parenting Order (without consent) without reality testing or future pacing and a property and financial split in favour of one of the parents, to the tune of 70:30 or 60:40 depending on the number of children and who they reside with.

Both parents' relationships as partners is surely over, now very bitter, their communication sounds harsh, sometimes non-existent. Their parenting style changed into a conflicting parenting style, as opposed to a parallel or cooperative one. Neither parent believes it is in their children's best interest, but they have an Order, and the case has been closed … pay up parents, hope you can implement the Court Order or else hope the conflicts do not keep on affecting your lives, for the sake of your children.

There have been many parents who have found the Court Orders were unworkable and have come to FDR to have these revised through FDR as liveable Parenting Plans which are now recognised by the Australian Family's and Federal Magistrate's Courts, converting them to Parenting Orders by Consent.

Separated parents going through litigation can become quite hostile towards each other as they have spent thousands of dollars and initially did not wish to litigate. In some cases, one set of grandparents will offer to pay for the litigation costs. After the lost court outcome some become smarter, wiser, and slightly poorer, none the less they are more interested in the best interest of their children. They often wake up to the reality that they are the best people on earth to determine what is best for their own children.

They wish to be assisted in this discussion to develop agreement by trained experts and highly experienced professionals, who have the best interest of their children in mind. We offer co-mediation within one week or two, with a 100% money back quality guarantee. It is provided face-to-face and via Zoom now, as a gender balanced process (female and male mediator) and continues to deliver great outcomes, which all can live with and afford.

My colleagues say I am a compliance-focused, detail-oriented, and highly organised Mediator/Investigator/Trainer, with extensive experience leading complex and sensitive investigations as well as dispute management.

I know my thorough research, superior critical thinking, and sound judgement facilitates evidence-based decision making to draw informed conclusions and recommendations. Applying excellent attention to detail and written communication qualities, I prepare comprehensive and accurate submissions, case reports, statements, Parenting Plans, and Brief of Evidence.

Q How do you find Jean-Marcel?

Mobile: +61 0419 253 762

Email: Marcel@InvestigationandMediation.com.au

Website: www.InvestigationandMediation.com.au

Q What happens when you contact us?

You will receive a **FREE Consultation** and book an appointment if appropriate.

Q What happens when you book an appointment for an Initial Assessment?

1. Pre-Pay Invoice.
2. One-hour confidential session.
3. Contact made with other party by FDRP.
4. Joint Session is arranged, after initial assessments with each party, if appropriate.

I am highly organised, plan efficiently and prioritise competing workloads, completing tasks to resolution within tight timeframes. I have helped many parents over the past two decades having provided more than three thousand mediations, I am recognised to have the following:

KEY STRENGTHS

- *Extensive experience preparing and conducting complex investigations across a wide variety of areas, utilising a comprehensive understanding of contemporary best practice investigations processes and practices.*

- *Proven background across complex case management, develops tailored care plans for people from diverse cultural and socio-economic backgrounds to cater for their individual needs.*

- *Demonstrated knowledge of all legislative procedures including legislative breaches, regulatory frameworks, and Court proceedings.*

- *Strong negotiator; develops and consolidates excellent working relationships with a variety of internal and external stakeholder groups.*

- *Outstanding verbal communication skills, including the preparation of detailed oral reports, resulting in rapidly developing commitment, trust, and responsiveness across a range of networks.*

- *Highly developed analytical and problem-solving qualities; develops innovative solutions to emerging issues, utilising strong judgement and evidence-based decision-making.*

- *Superior attention to detail and written communications skills facilitating the production and delivery of high-quality reports, evidentiary briefs, and statements.*

- *Excellent organisational and time management, prioritising urgent and complex workloads to meet strict deadlines and ensure tasks adhere to quality standards.*

Jean-Marcel Malliaté MDR

InterMEDIATE Dispute Management

Master of Dispute Resolution

Fellow Resolutions Institute

Member of Alternative Dispute Resolution Association ADRA

Nationally Accredited Family Dispute Resolution Practitioner

Ph: 0419 253 762

E: marcel@investigationandmediation.com.au

CERTIFICATIONS AND LICENSES

Master of Dispute Resolution 2002 (Law Faculty UTS)
- Commercial & Private Investigator (NSW, Police CAPI Lic: 411750343 Master's Licence 981-371-90S)

Security Operations (SLED, NSW Police Master's Licence 000 258 693)
Private Security & Investigator (Victorian Police: 981-371-90S)
Cert IV Investigation Government Agencies 2018 -2019 (ICETS)
Cert IV in Leadership & Management 2016 - 2017 (Learning Management Australia)
Cert 111 Investigation Services - NSW Government (CPP 30607)
Grad Dip Family Dispute Resolution 2010 Interrelate Family Centre
Adv Dip Appl Social Science 1998 (Aust College of Applied Psychology)
Dip Counselling & Communication 1996 (ACAP)
Current Working with Children's Check (Aust Federal Police)
Drone/Aerial Investigation Specialist (CASA: ARN1083319)

Head Office: Carlingford, U12-1, Level/3, 372 Pennant Hills Rd, Carlingford NSW 2118

8
COME FLY WITH ME ... ON A DC-3

by JOY ALLARDYCE

"Better five minutes late than dead on time!"

(Displayed in the Brisbane TAA Pilot's Crew Room)

Queensland 1953. We were on the return leg of flight 486/487 Mount Isa, Cloncurry, Julia Creek, Richmond, Hughenden, Charters Towers, Townsville after leaving Mount Isa at 0630 (6.30am). It was mid-January, and the summer heat was intense. The DC-3 was continually buffeted by up drafts fed by the ground heat and passengers were not travelling well.

Descending into Hughenden on the hop from Richmond the turbulence increased, so I checked that everyone was wearing seatbelts in compliance with the "Fasten Seatbelt" sign switched on by the captain.

If the "No Smoking" sign had also been activated, I too would need to be strapped in. However, I was standing at the rear of the cabin, keeping an eye on the passengers when a man in a forward seat stood up.

He stumbled towards me clinging to the seats as his body swayed with the motion of the aircraft – I assumed he was heading to the lavatory. When he drew level with me and we were face-to-face, I asked, "Can I help you?" He opened his mouth to speak, but unfortunately, no words escaped just a steady stream of vomit! I copped the lot!

"Please be seated," I gasped, "we will be landing soon. There are sick bags in the pocket of the seat in front of you." Without a word, he turned and staggered back to his seat. A bottle of soda water partially cleaned my uniform, even so, the smell lingered for the remainder of the flight and the tram ride home.

© Excerpt from *Come Fly With Me ... On A DC-3* by Joy Allardyce

> *Go confidently in the direction of your dreams. Live the life you've imagined."*
> — **Henry David Thoreau**

So much has changed in the aviation industry since 1952. Larger, faster aircraft bring overseas destinations within reach of all Australians who have the travel bug.

We no longer have Air Hostesses (hosties), they have become Flight Attendants, and passengers' dress mode has fallen from stylish fashions for females and suits with shirt and tie for males (except for destinations such as Darwin or Northern Queensland when just a shirt and tie sufficed) into casual wear.

These days we are more inclined to see passengers wearing jeans and shorts complemented by the dreaded flip flops which are great for the beach but somewhat irksome and unattractive for aircraft travel. At least in the case of an emergency ditching in the ocean, we would not have to worry about spiked heels penetrating the exit chute or the life raft!

I hope you, the reader, enjoyed this story of the early Air Hostesses and the intrepid DC-3. How lucky I was to be able to see this vast, stunning land of ours; how lucky to make such wonderful friends and meet people from different states, different walks of life and different countries all because of the "good old DC-3 days".

My book was motivated by all the wonderful memories I had of those heady flying days, and the long-lasting friendships formed while flying in Queensland and southern states, including Tasmania, as well as the Northern Territory.

It was written with pride for an organisation that reached so many people, not only those on or near the eastern seaboard but also those resilient souls who lived in the Outback regions where isolation can be likened to living on an island.

Instead of the surrounding ocean lapping at the shoreline or damaging, ferocious cyclones that tear at trees and demolish buildings, nature conjures up destructive dust storms and swirling willy-willies that breathe red dust over everything that stands in their path. These resourceful Outback people have big hearts while their homesteads and towns are simply microscopic dots in the vast land that encompasses their boundaries.

Trans-Australia Airlines (TAA), a government-owned organisation, the trading name of the Australian National Airlines Commission, commenced operation in February 1946. In June of that year, wrote Sir Hudson Fysh in his book *Wings to the World*, Lester Brain began work as General Manager with John Borthwick as his personal assistant and Doug Laurie on the traffic side. Three months later, TAA's first flight was made on a DC-3 from Melbourne to Sydney.

On the 2nd of April 1949, in Brisbane, TAA acquired the Queensland and Northern Territory Aerial Services (Qantas) routes serviced by Qantas Empire Airways (QEA) and this acquisition also included the Flying Doctor Service, now known as the Royal Flying Doctor Service (RFDS).

Fast forward 46 years to the 9th of September 1992, when there was a re-enactment of TAA's first FLIGHT.

Fast forward another 29 years and aviation as we know it, has been sidelined to row upon row of hundreds of jet planes parked on runways in moth balls in countries all over the world. Waiting their return to the skies when international borders re-open and flights return to normal carrying capacity as the world labours under the economic decline of the Covid-19 pandemic.

In 2021, all commercial passenger flights have ground to a halt. The pandemic has up ended the aviation industry. Freight flights now take to the skies in a bid to keep some semblance of international trade afloat. Families caught in far off countries returning home under quarantine slowly fill our hotels and return to their loved ones with stories of despair and great sadness.

History will always offer stories of fortune and hardship, but despite all of this, the Australian aviation industry, clings by the seat of its pants and waits breathless for a return to the skies once more.

ABOUT THE AUTHOR

JOY ALLARDYCE

Come Fly With Me ... On a DC-3

TAA Air Hostess in the late 1950's, Joy wrote her book at the grand age of 89!

Definitely a book worth reading about the history of commercial aviation in the 1950s.

Find Joy's book at www.tracytully.com

9

LOST AT SEA! CALIBRATE YOUR MINDSET … FIND TRUE NORTH

by TRACY TULLY

" *It is not the critic who counts; not the person who points out how the strong man stumbles, or where the doer of deeds could have done them better.*

The credit belongs to the man who is actually in the arena, whose face is marred by dust and sweat and blood; who strives valiantly; who errs, who comes short again and again, because there is no effort without error and shortcoming; but who does actually strive to do the deeds; who knows great enthusiasms, the great devotions; who spends himself in a worthy cause; who at the best knows in the end the triumph of high achievement, and who at the worst, if he fails, at least fails while daring greatly, so that his place shall never be with those cold and timid souls who neither know victory nor defeat"

— **Henry David Thoreau**

Have you ever felt fear when you've been trapped in a difficult situation?

You can't move because you're frozen with fear?

That feeling when you know, there's no turning back.

I have when I was lost at sea.

I learned how to **Buckle Up Fear** that day.

Do you know that empty pit in your stomach?

When your heart's pumping so hard, that it feels like it's going to burst?

That sick feeling of dread when you realize that your worst nightmare is about to come true.

That's exactly how I felt the day I was lost at sea.

Fear is triggered by a threat of danger, it's a survival mechanism that causes fight or flight and for some, they freeze.

Fear makes us feel scared and anxious.

I've found that 1:5 men and 1:7 women in Australia feel anxiety, according to the 2020 Australian Bureau of Statistics ABS.

Who starts breathing rapidly when they're scared?

I do and especially when I'm scuba diving.

My breathing rate rises rapidly, and I use up a lot of air in my tank.

I've learned to slow my breathing rate down by inhaling deep breaths in through the nose and out through my mouth.

Come for a dive underwater with me. Close your eyes.

Breathe slowly. Imagine you are 60 feet underwater, 18 metres down in shadowy darkness.

The water is cold, dark, and eerie.

Concentrate on looking ahead, try to see what's in front of you.

The ocean is empty. There's nothing. Only stillness.

Around you it's dim and gloomy, the water is dull and a murky grey.

You think you can see objects close by, but you can't make anything out clearly.

It's just you in a vast, silent ocean.

All you can hear is your breathing as the regulator supplies you with precious air.

When you breathe out, the bubbling sound interrupts the silence.

As you slowly descend, the water gets colder.

You can feel the icy sea surrounding your body through your diving suit.

Breathe slowly. Breathe in and out.

Now open your eyes.

The Australian PADI Diving Association tells us that we must always dive with a buddy.

For some reason, no one joined me that day.

It was the 12th of December 1984, and I was sitting in a boat in the ocean at the Mackay Harbour.

I was completing my scuba diving certificate with my final Open Sea Dive.

My instructions – dive down, set my coordinates, swim until I found an anchor, climb up and pass the course.

If I didn't, I failed.

Then I had to ascend, fill my vest with air from the tank and swim back to the boat. I had saved for half a year for this trip, travelling thousands of kilometres to get to the course location.

There was no way I was going to fail that day.

I remember we were rushing as a cyclone was heading our way. I was the last diver into the water.

I jumped in from the boat, my weights felt heavy, and I grabbed at the anchor chain to slow me down, using precious air in my clumsy descent.

That action sealed my fate that day, forcing me to learn how to **Buckle Up Fear**.

Hanging onto the anchor, I set my compass coordinates, before swimming off into the dark water.

I swam in silence, all the time searching around me for an anchor chain.

Fifteen minutes into my dive, I noticed uninvited guests on my left side.

Several venomous sea snakes had joined me.

Slowly turning to the right, I saw the whole colony!

How would you feel if you found yourself swimming with sea snakes?

My heart raced; I began breathing quickly. Thoughts raced through my head … what if I was bitten?

With no buddy to swim for help.

It wouldn't matter anyway, there wouldn't be enough time to save me.

Fear prepares us to react to danger by shutting down functions not needed for survival and sharpens our major senses that help us to survive, such as our eyesight.

My eyes were wide open that day!

I needed to conserve my oxygen and **Buckle Up Fear**.

I learned how to **Buckle Up Fear** that day, by using a **3 STEP Method**:

1. **ASSESS and breathe slowly.**
2. **ADAPT and prepare.**
3. **ACT first, analyse later.**

Halfway into the dive, I noticed I was heading into deeper water.

How could that be?

Was this the test or was I lost?

Surely not?

Oh no! Not lost at sea!

I started panicking, doubt crept in.

This was real, it was happening to me.

I was lost in the ocean, no diving buddy and with little air left in my tank.

It was too late to go back, so I decided to keep swimming.

Focusing on slowing my breathing, I desperately searched for an anchor.

The air in my tank was running low.

When tackling a challenging task, you need purpose and determination.

My purpose was to stay alive; I wasn't going to fail this dive at any cost.

So, I kept swimming.

Have you ever felt sheer fear? I did that day.

Imagine you're all alone in the ocean.

This is when I learned the power to **Buckle Up Fear**.

When you **Buckle Up Fear**, you focus on survival.

Our heart rate increases and blood flows to the muscles, so we can move faster.

I chose to **Buckle Up Fear** and kept swimming.

My air tank level was getting low when finally, an anchor appeared ahead in front of me.

I'd made it! I was so relieved.

I pulled myself up the anchor chain and climbed onto the back of the boat.

I stood up, purging the air from my regulator noisily, making a satisfying whooshing sound, spraying water everywhere. It felt so good, such a relief.

Clearing my mask so I could see, I looked up.

It wasn't my boat and not my instructor either.

Two shocked people were staring at me and by the looks on their faces, I was not welcome onboard.

I pushed my mask up and removed my mouthpiece to speak.

Hastily I tried to explain my situation, but the woman started screaming.

She screamed and screamed, a horrified look on her face.

The guy picked up something from the bottom of the boat.

I looked closely, he was holding a hook and brandishing it in my direction.

I couldn't believe what was happening to me!

It was like a James Bond movie, and I was the villain.

I had no time to explain and fearing for my life again, I launched back into the water, inflating my vest with the last air in my tank.

Looking at the beach in the distance, I spotted the boat I was supposed to find. A speck on the water. And I was in shark infested waters.

I didn't waste any time, swimming as fast as I could straight back to our boat.

When you **Buckle Up Fear** it gives you time to ASSESS the situation and breathe.

My situation taught me to **Buckle Up Fear** and swim back to the safety of the beach.

Today I want to teach you how to **Buckle Up Fear** when you find yourself in a tough situation.

To help you **Buckle Up Fear**, you can use my **3 STEP Method**:

1. **ASSESS and breathe slowly.**

2. **ADAPT and prepare.**

3. **ACT first, analyse later.**

Over the years I've often thought about that couple fishing on the boat.

I bet they tell all their friends at dinner parties about the day a diver dressed in black climbed out of the sea and jumped into the back of their boat!

I can just imagine it; the couple would be entertaining their friends with their amazing story.

Who would have thought that I would find their anchor in the middle of the ocean?

It was like finding a needle in a haystack!

But one thing I know for sure …

My **Buckle Up Fear 3 STEP METHOD** kept me alive that day and could help you too.

Best wishes,

Tracy Tully

SPEAKER BIO

Ranked in the Courier Mail's **POWER LIST: TOP 50 Most Influential People in Education**; Tracy Tully dominates conversations at state, national and international levels; influencing decisions that matter in education and training.

Winner of the global **BUSINESS xCellance AWARDS 2023 Coaching Women Category,** Tracy is an Author, Keynote Speaker, TV, and Media personality. In 2023 she added a small boutique book publishing provider to her suite of services and started her Legacy Project working with ex-service Australian Women Veterans publishing a collaborative Co-Author book.

With a career spanning over 40 years in education, leadership, and training, she fearlessly swapped her school principal whistle becoming a 'corruption whistleblower' in a nation built on British penal colonies, with a formidable '*Tall Poppy Syndrome*' culture.

Tracy entered the domain of those who really can *'tell it like it is,'* presenting the real facts, even if it's unpleasant; setting the record straight when she published her book:

FEARless Buckle Up ... Build RESILIENCE, leaving 'no stone unturned.'

Tracy is a coach and on the job **Leadership Solutions Specialist** influencing frontline leadership capability and productivity guiding leaders to grow their motivation and resilience, by demonstrating how to overcome fear and procrastination through her **3 Step BUCKLE UP FEAR Method – Assess, Adapt and Act.**

She trains leaders and workforce teams to build communication, develop resilience, grow their team work, have accountability and ownership and how to deal with difficult people in an ever-changing complex world.

Tracy helps employers with those difficult conversations they don't want to have through her two step **SHIFT and LIFT** process:

1. **SHIFT** employees through termination

2. **LIFT** employees by managing unsatisfactory performance

Holding senior leadership roles in the public, private and non-profit sectors for the last four decades, Tracy is renowned for her strategic and innovative problem solving.

ABOUT THE AUTHOR

TRACY TULLY

A Motivation percolator and distiller of fear; Tracy turns chaos into calm and overwhelm into power and passion. Book a 1:1 session at www.tracytully.com.

Under the banner www.tracytully.com Tracy is a purveyor of inspiration and Jill-of-all Trades in mastering fear, building courage, and strengthening resilience; her key message being:

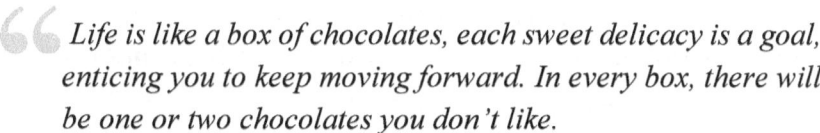
Life is like a box of chocolates, each sweet delicacy is a goal, enticing you to keep moving forward. In every box, there will be one or two chocolates you don't like.

I will show you how to find the sweet spot in everything you do!

Most of the battle is in achieving the right mindset."
—***Tracy Tully***

KEYNOTE SPEAKER

Tracy challenges people to step out of their comfort zone by building their resilience.

Conducting powerful and witty speaking opportunities, Tracy teaches people how to grow self-confidence through her **3 Step BUCKLE UP FEAR Method**: strengthening resilience and motivation by adopting a positive mindset.

Her presentations are passionate and highly engaging, guaranteeing you'll never forget her. "I can show you how to find the sweet spot in how you think and in everything you do!"

SPEAKING TOPIC: Lost at Sea - Calibrate your Mindset & Find True North **– Tracy shares her 3 Step BUCKLE UP FEAR Method demonstrating how to build resilience by getting comfortable with fear.**

Testimonials:

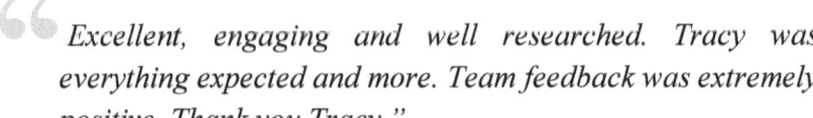
> *Excellent, engaging and well researched. Tracy was everything expected and more. Team feedback was extremely positive. Thank you Tracy."*
> *— **Simon Knight AkzoNobel***

" *I found Tracy after doing a little online search for someone who could speak on the topics of resilience, fear, and change management. After a brief introductory call, I knew Tracy was the right fit for our franchise partner event. As a first for our brand, we brought together franchisees who were experiencing change at a large organisational level. Tracy was committed to our mission and went above and beyond to learn about our business. She attended our studios to ensure she could grasp the 'lingo' and met with key players ahead of time. Tracy delivered at every touch point. Not only is she an engaging speaker, but she also had our group working together and that was the magical moment for me. Thank you Tracy, for your total commitment. You're an absolute rockstar."*

— **Natasha Borgatti Celebrity Ink**

AUTHOR

Author of **FEARless Buckle Up ... Build RESILIENCE** Tracy is a courageous whistle blower detailing her true-life experiences, explaining why there's no room for assumptions, blame or procrastination.

Publishing a collection of co-author books, Tracy provides a unique mentoring experience for those who don't have the time or confidence to write a book. Offering an exclusive opportunity to dip their pens into the delightful world of wordsmithing, through collaboration with likeminded people, she empowers them to become co-authors through writing a chapter. You are reading one of her co-author books now!

An accomplished children's author, Tracy entertains children with Australian stories for kids of all ages. *Gordon the Goat and the Gully Kids* was based on a real-life story and created at the large silky oak dining room table during school holidays, with her kids contributing to the pages as the book grew. Gordon grew up on a station in far southwest Queensland.

Renowned Australian artist and illustrator, Sean Leahy brings her stories characters to life with his hilarious cartoons, sharing her lovable book character's antics.

Purchase her book here: www.tracytully.com/fearless/

For Speaker Bookings and bulk book sale enquiries:

+61 429 992 916
coauthorbooks@gmail.com
www.tracytully.com

Connect with Tracy on Social Media:

- facebook.com/mrwcoaching
- instagram.com/motivationresilienceforwomen/
- pinterest.com.au/motivatingresil/
- linkedin.com/in/tracy-tully-3879a2122/

SHE RISES FROM THE FIRE

A HEROIC PROSE

"*It's not the words of man that count, it's the words of women too; not those who **deceive** and delight in the failure of others, never experiencing triumph or defeat.*

The praise belongs to the woman who fights the fire, rising burnt and scarred; refusing to fear her critics. The one who navigates floods, cliffs and roadblocks, facing corrupt, masked highwaymen at gunpoint.

The woman who watches, when they cut the rope of safety smiling smugly, as she plunges into the abyss.

The tribute in fact, belongs to the woman who feels the terror and trepidation of what's invisible around the corner, who suffers the pain when she gets it wrong but has the strength to pursue, because without effort, there is no failure.

She is the one who stands strong in turbulence, who struggles unaided making mistakes, who bravely travels alone.

They are the fake ones; unmotivated, dishonest, claiming their glory from those with passion; who do good deeds and have experienced the victory of great achievement.

For SHE fears less and dares to challenge them all."
—***Tracy Tully 23 April 2019***

Inspired by *Man In The Arena* speech by Theodore Roosevelt, US President, 23 April 1910.

BECOME A CO-AUTHOR!

Have you ever dreamed of becoming a published author?

If you have secretly harboured the thought of seeing your name in print, then the MRW 90 Day Co- Author Program is for you!

Collaborate with other likeminded people and write a chapter of 3,000 to 5,000 words, with others.

Every chapter has the power to turn the narrative into conversations, which in turn grows your profile and influence.

If you're an established business owner and you've always wanted to become a published author but lack the confidence or are too time poor to write a whole book, then this is the program for you!

It takes just 3 steps to write your chapter and includes a fun training program in Sales and Marketing to make your bank account tinkle with the sound of dollars, generating money while you sleep!

My promise to you is NO piles of boxes full of books in the garage collecting dust! We'll show you how to leverage a great network of other authors to scale your business.

Become an author and business partner in this dream of yours… publish your own book with MRW Publishing!

Connect with Tracy:

Call or **text** me on +61 429 992 916

Web: www.tracytully.com

Email: coauthorbooks@gmail.com

www.ingramcontent.com/pod-product-compliance
Lightning Source LLC
Chambersburg PA
CBHW031249290426
44109CB00012B/504